SANATAN SANGH PARIVAR

TWENTY FOUR HOUR TWELVE HOUR- ONE HOUR

Written by

KANHAIYA JEE ANAND, AMIE,MBA

SHARDA KUMARI, PGDM (Human Rights)

BEDATRI ANAND, B.ARCH

UTKARS ANAND, B.ARCH

Title : Sanatan Sangh Parivar
(Twenty Four Hour-Twelve Hour- One Hour

Author : Kanhaiya Jee Anand, Sharda Kumari,
Bedatri Anand, Utkars Anand

Edition : First (June, 2024)

ISBN : 9788197599668

Published by

A Venture by -
PRACHI DIGITAL PUBLICATION

Regd. Add.: 254, Khuriyakhatta No. 10, Bindukhatta,
Lalkuan, Nainital - 262402, Uttarakhand, India
Website : www.taneeshapublishers.in
E-mail : taneeshapublishers@gmail.com
Phone : +91 845481 2712, +91 976041 7980

Printed by :
Manipal Technologies Limited, Bengaluru - 560001, Karnataka

DEDICATION

This book is dedicated to Budhavtar Jagatguru Shankracharya Puri Mahabhag, All Shankracharya, Acharya, All Judges, Rastriya Swam Sevak Sangh, Engineer Live Foundation, All Math Mandir, All Institution, Mother Draupdi Devi and all family members.

PREFACE

Word of Buddha Avtar Jagat Guru Shankaracharya Puri Mahabhag - Compulsory devote one hour to your Street temple/Society and deposit one rupees in temple/Society trust daily, and if you are eligible deposit 10 rupees for 9 more family who is not eligible means 1 hour and 10 rupees daily to Street temple will not only enrich the temple it will create strong and rich street Math Mandir. 100% Math and Mandir created by the group of Local public who given the Land, Created Building and run the Institution. More than 90% School, College and Institution which is based on Macale theory and based on Church education system is also created by the Public itself even initially this was run by group of Local people and they are teaching the Ramayana, Geeta also but due to poor word in constitution whole system is disturbed by the Greedy political Karyakarta, in today political Karyakarta created a rules to get tax directly from people and they are spending in name of social welfare without touching to the person who created and Mahant of the Math Mandir , who created and Acharya of the School, college and various institution in country. Few team is attached with Political karyakarta is under depression. This is required to change the condition in country.

Who is the Human being in world who does not living in Sanatan Sangha.

All Human being like to live in Sanatan Sangha it may be of Tea party Sangha, Card playing Sangh, Drinker Sangha, kawariya sangha, Budha Sangha, jain Sangha, Likely minded people Sangha, Rastriya Swamsevak sangha. Political Party Sangha. Family Sangha, Sadhu and sant Sangha.

Hence we can say that Society is ruled by Sanatan Sangha.

Single person can control own and creating Family to marry with opposite sex and Women controlling the house, Few family staying one place and to fulfill the needs of each other creating Street Sanatan temple/Sanatan society and Sanatan Sant, Mahatma who creating Sanatan Sangha and controlling the Sanatan Society of various number of family.

Sanatan Sangh starting once number of family staying one place, Sanatan Sangha controlling the various family through Sanatan Temple. Further it takes the shape of village - Communities - Jila - State - Country - World.

People devoting 24 hours for their own and 12 hour for family.

Voluntarily People spending hour for discussion with others regarding own problem, family problem and society problem at certain places.

Needs creating the work of 12 hour, some are voluntarily some are on payment spending their 12 hours for others work.

Whole World is a Ayurved, we are Ayurved, You are Ayurved, Every Women is a Universe, where life taking place or which is the reason of Birth, a mother of Ayurved and Street Temple is the Open Laboratory of Ayurved. Every element whether this should be in form of Sound, Touchment, vision, taste and smell is from the family of Ayurved.

Every Element including Zero, tree plant including all Creatures taking birth in form of vibration from Zero and vibration takes place when sound developing reason of Akash created by the Param Brahma (in form of Zero Element) which can not be destroyed.

In zero Vibration taking shape of dead cell and dead cell to live cell in women worm.

Child living in worm without water, food, air and environment but attached with Navel and when child come out from Worm, child starting to respire and when starting child crying further child growing on mother milk for minimum of 6 to 24 months.

Further slowly slowly child taking food, water etc. In one to two year child starting to walk and talk and slowly slowly child taking their shape of body till 10 to 12 years.

Later age reaching to 20 - 30 - 40 - 50 - 60 - 70 - 80 - 90 - 100 and so on and various changing takes place includes self control technique, creating of family and house to develop the family and few family in specific area. Creating Sanatan Temple/Society to establish either in form of Sound, touchment, vision, taste and smell in form of sound creation such as meditation or watching self sound or movement of air on hill station or bank of river etc or Lighting in form of sun, agni or in sense of taste in form of River, sea, pond or in sense of various smell means in form of Soil, Pind, Murti, statue due to integration effect of vibration.

Continuous movement bringing the all types of natural energy in short while.

The every element have own life cycle till differentiating to the vibration and zero.

This is the basic concept of Sanatan Sangha Pariwar - Twenty Four hour - Twelve hour - One Hour.

CONTENTS

Who is Dandi Sanyasi?

Meaning of Dandi Sanyasi:

The Word Dandi means Danda or stick, which is a symbol of discipline, and sanyasi means one who withdraws from external involvement in worldly life. The scriptures also refer to the Danda as 'Brahma Danda, ' symbolizing Bhagawan Vishnu.

What is JAGATGURU?

JAGATGURU is the person who is a symbol of Truth, who either dictating or who written Bhasya on Geeta, Upnishad and Brahmsutra.

Who is Acharya?

An acharya is a formal title of a teacher or guru, who has attained a degree in Veda and Vedanga.

Seven Acharya is as under -

Adi Sankaracharya - Shankaracharya is a religious title used by the heads of amnaya monasteries called mathas in the Advaita Vedanta tradition.

Adi Shankara, also called Adi Shankaracharya, was an Indian Vedic scholar and teacher. His works present a harmonizing reading of the sastras, with liberating knowledge of the self at its core, synthesizing the

Advaita Vedanta teachings of his time.

Shankaracharya travelled in and through the land of Bharata for reestablishing the Vaidika Dharma which was in the verge of losing all its importance. His effort in unifying the Bharata by establishing various mathas and other centres has saved Bharata from losing its spiritual treasures.

Ramanujacharya - Ramanuja, also known as Ramanujacharya, was an Indian Hindu philosopher, guru and a social reformer. He is noted to be one of the most important exponents of the Sri Vaishnavism tradition within Hinduism. His philosophical foundations for devotionalism were influential to the Bhakti movement.

Madhvacharya - Madhvāchārya, and also known as Purna Prajna and Ānanda Tīrtha, was an Indian philosopher, theologian and the chief proponent of the Dvaita school of Vedanta. Madhva called his philosophy Tattvavāda meaning "arguments from a realist viewpoint".

Nimbarkacharya - Nimbarkacharya, also known as Nimbarka, Nimbaditya or Niyamananda, was a Hindu philosopher, theologian and the chief proponent of the theology of Dvaitadvaita or dualistic–non - dualistic.

Vallabhacharya - Vallabhācārya, also known as Vallabha, was an Indian saint and philosopher. He founded the Krishna - centered Puṣṭimārga sect of Vaishnavism in the Braj region of India, and propounded the philosophy of Śuddhādvaita. Vallabha was born in a Telugu Tailang Brahmin family that was residing in Varanasi.

Chaitanya Mahaprabhu - Chaitanya Mahaprabhu was a 15th - century Indian Hindu saint from Bengal who is considered to be the combined avatar of Radha and Krishna by his disciples and various scriptures. Chaitanya Mahaprabhu's mode of worshipping Krishna with bhajan - kirtan and dance had a profound effect on Vaishnavism in Bengal.

Acharya Sandipani - Guru of Krishna and Balarama . He is regarded to have educated them regarding all the Vedas, the art of drawing, astronomy, gandharva veda, medicine, training elephants and horses, and archery.

What is Vedanga.

The six Vedangas are Siksha, Chhanda, Vyakarana, Nirukta, Jyotisha and Kalpa.

VEDANGA	LIMBS COMPARED WITH
Chandah	Legs
Kalpa	Hands
Jyotisa	Eyes
Nirukta	Ears
Siksha	Nose
Vyakaranam	Face

The six Vedaṅgas or 'Limbs of the Vedas'			Upa-Vedas
1. Śikṣā		Phonetics	Āyur-Veda (Health)
2. Chandas		Prosody	Dhanur Veda (Archery)
3. Vyāvakaraṇa :–		Grammar	Śastra-śāstra (Martial Arts)
	Aṣṭhādhyāyī	By Pāṇini	Gāndharva-Veda (Music)
	Dhātu-pāṭha		Sthāpatya-Veda (Architecture)
	Gaṇa- pāṭha		Śilpa-śāstra (Fine Arts)
	Lingānuśāsana		
	Śikṣā		**Ṣaḍ-darśana**
4. Nirukta		Etymology (by Yāska)	Mīmāṃsa Sūtras (Jaimini)
5. Jyotiśa		Astronomy/Astrology	Nyāya Sūtras (Gautama)
6. Kalpa	Śrauta sūtra	Ritual	Saṅkhya Sūtras (Kapila)
	Smārta sutra:–		Vaiśeṣika Sūtras (Kaṇāḍa)
	• Grihya-sūtras		Yoga Sūtras (Patañjali)
	• Dharma-sūtras		Vedānta Sūtras (Bādarāyaṇa)

What is Veda?

Shruti /The Vedas
Rig Veda
Yajur Veda
Sama Veda
Atharva Veda
Karma Kanda
Jnana Kanda
Samhitas
Brahmanas
Aranyakas
Upanishads
(Poetic) Mantras, Hymns Chanting
(Prose) Rituals, Sacrificial rites, Explanations
Simplified Rituals (at forest), secret rituals, philosophical analysis of rites, more contemplation on philosophy
Vedanta (End of vedic knowledge), Discussions on Brahman, Jivatma-Paramatma unity, no more rituals
hinduismwayoflife.com

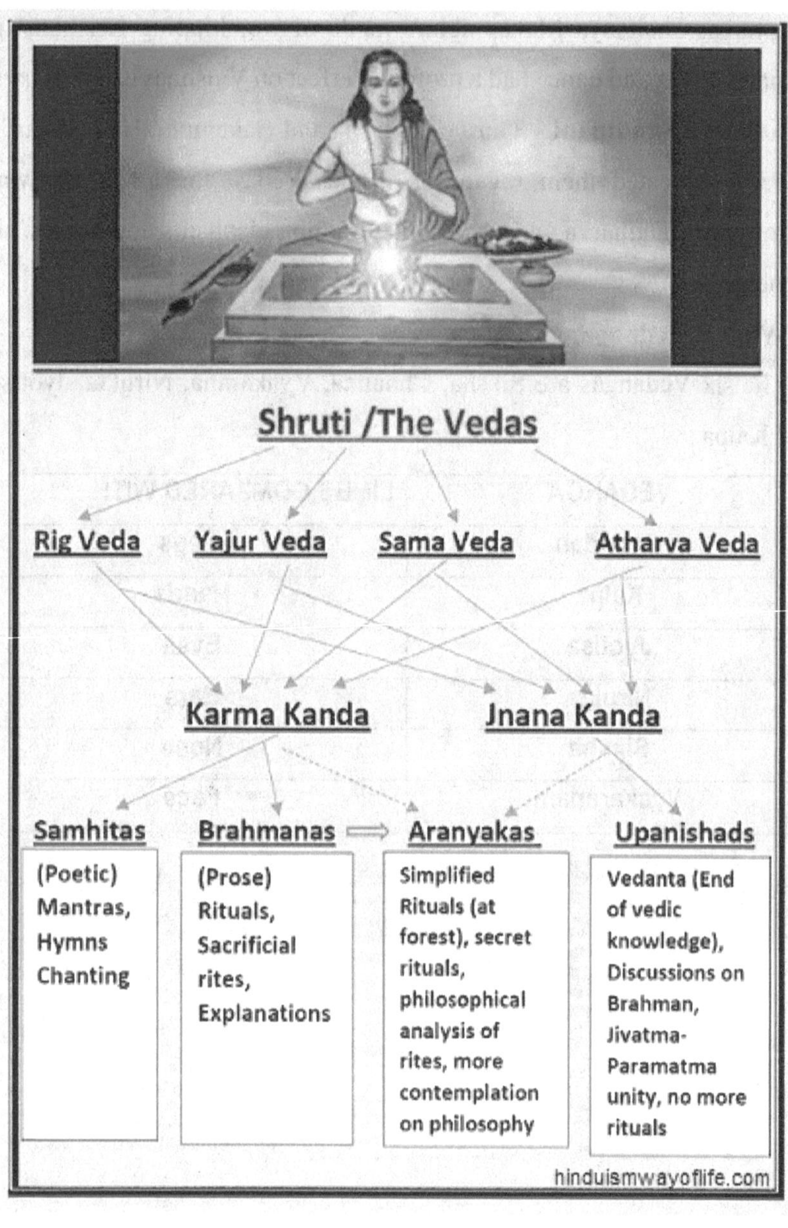

Hinduism – Scriptures & Philosophies

(Click at each sub - title below to read more)

The Shrutis (Vedas)

The Smritis

Prasthana Triya

– Vedanta – Upanishads

– Bhagavad Gita

– Brahma Sutras (Uttara Mimamsa)

Dharma Shastras

4 Purusharthas

– Dharma

– Artha

– Kama

– Moksha

Darshan Shastras

– Poorva Mimamsa

– Nyaya

– Vaiseshika

– Sankhya

3 schools of philosophy regarding Soul & God

– Dvaita (Dualism)

– Visitadvaita (Qualified non - dualism)

– Advaita (Non - dualism)

Agama Shastra

Yogas

– Bhakti Yoga

– Gnyana Yoga

– Karma Yoga

– Raja Yoga

– Pathanjali Yoga Sutras

– Kundalini Yoga

– Hatha Yoga

Yoga Vasishta

Panchadasi

Ayuveda

Jyotisha

Various Concepts & Tenets

Creation

Brahman – God beyond name & Form

– Sat - Chit - Ananda

Soul, Atman & Brahman

Body - Mind - Intellect - Ego - Atman

Vasanas - Tendencies

Goal of Human Life

Karma & Rebirth

Trigunas - Satva Rajas Tamas - 3

3 States of awareness

– Jagrat (Waking)

– Swapna (Dream sleep)

– Sushupti (Dreamless sleep)

– Turiya – the 4th state

Samsara Cycle

– Birth, Living, death

– Reincarnation/ rebirth

Mukti, Moksha, Liberation

– Jeevan Mukta

– God realization/ Self realization

Thirukkural (Tamil)

The Gospel of Sri Ramakrishna

Bhagwan Ramana Maharshi's 'Naanaar?" (Who am I?)

Bhagvan Ramana Maharshi's Upadesa Saram, Ullathu Narpathu etc

CASE STUDY - 1

Human being started life from Jungle, Initially Human being was living alone and at needs of Women joining each other.

Time started Women and Men was started to stay at one place to help the Children to grow.

Men and Women is working and earning, constructing of their house, living together day and night etc.

In morning and in evening gathering one place and gossiping together.

Some are performing business, some have work in their own surroundings, some have work in Land, keeping Cow, Ox etc and living together in family, but before going to work and after coming work talking or gossiping together.

This gossiping identity the some place where people are sitting either under tree or at river bank or on hill or on land. Few people are taking interest and forming a committee to construct the Temple where people are gathering for help to the other members.

In my village Hasanpur more than 200 families live together.

Mostly are self dependent either they are doing their own business or agriculture etc.

Women are working inside of House.

Children living with Parents.

Almost all houses have cows and Land.

There is two temples, Playground, Football ground, volleyball ground, Exercise house, One Library and one school in Village constructed by own to share the free few hour and money to this work by villagers.

In Present due to lack of technical knowledge temple is utilised by Women to have their own puja and others.

This is not now much effective place of learning from moring to evening previously this was.

Village does not have any bank, previously some one have more money and they are behaving like lender and circulating the money in between.

Villages itself producing the vegetable, crops and utilising each other to share the things each other, while surplus moving to local market for sell.

Morning and Evening mostly Women are going to Temple and performing Puja to keep their health update.

Evening and Morning Man also moving to Temple for Puja and Gossiping.

Group of Men are also engaging in Card playing work.

Villagers selecting their Mukhiya, Sarpanch etc for village work which are ineffective in work reason people who was not going to Court previously now going to Court for any Judgment.

Hospital and police station is also the availability in village for the health check up and safety but both places does not have any influence of discipline creation in society a serious concern. This is just a load from the Government on Society as village have few doctor ayurvedic, Homeopathy and allopathy is unutilised.

Performing business, agriculture and other activities is challenging and people spend more than 12 hours working together.

In Home mostly living together with family and working for family health and safety for 24 hours, while going to Temple, Library, Chauraha, Hospital, Police Station for Puja, for discussion, gossiping, Political, social, economic for health treatment, for safety for 1 hour etc.

Those who are devoting 24 hours to the work comes under the Twenty Four Hour such as Running the Self, Running the Business, Running the Industry, Activity of Sant, Sadhu, Muni, Rishi and Maharishi.

Working in Hospital, Working in School, Working in Industry, Working in Land, Working in Gaushala,

Business Centre is a good example of Twelve Hour. Human being joining the team to work in this category.

Tea Shop, Barber shop, Pan shop, Health center, wine shop, Temple, Library, Chauraha etc are the example of the One Hour.

Mostly people reaching these places to talk each other and knowing facts of each other, gossiping each other, in politics, economics, about village, country and world.

Every Individual in this world needs the requirement of Twenty Four Hour - Twelve Hour - One Hour.

Twenty Four hour is essential to grow in self,

A family man who is always living in form of Twelve Hour.

A house is dealt with by Twenty four hour responsibility.

A temple either in form of sky, air, heat, water & Earth

is run by the Pujari who is devoting Twenty four hour to the temple.

Every element in this world is the particle of GOD.

Business man, Guru, pandit, Scientist are devoting Twelve Hour for their work.

Those who are working for others, or serving voluntarily comes under the Twelve Hour.

People coming or going to organization, school, Hospital, factory, office, construction etc comes under the Twelve Hour.

Gossiping, talking, discussing every quality talk at Chauraha, Tea stall, Pan shop, Park regarding every quality comes under the One Hour.

Take the Example of SELF -

I am living in my own family with my wife, daughter, son and mother, elder family and younger family.

How my family will get food both time is our prime requirement, Secondly how my family is safe is the second most important requirement, while further how children should receive the higher quality of education is another important requirement in life, how my family should get a good health support. Our prime responsibility to establish our own work, such that family should work in same work.

Children should join the schooling to receive the best education.

How our family should involve in social politics.

For family talk, family thinking comes under the Twelve Hour.

While working in your own business with other helpers, joining school for education or teaching comes under the Twelve Hour.

Understanding of Social Politics, Marriage talk, Any function talk, any Yagya talk comes under the One Hour.

The Celebration of Durga Puja, Krishna ashtami, Ramayan Yagya comes under the product of One Hour.

School education is now deleterious due to outsider teacher, this teacher does not have capacity to teach a challenging. Mostly people want to send their children to the good English medium school, because now villagers does not have interest to teach,

Human body is the integration of the natural energy, when a human taking birth is just like a vibration forming a dead cell and reacting sukranu and converting to live cell on women worm. It integrates for 9 months without taking any direct food, water and respiration.

Child taking birth without respiration and ist respiration taking on earth.

On earth itself integrating the natural energy and continuously integrating the body and reaching to weight like 60 - 70 - 80 - 90 - 100 kg.

If the body gets the right energy as per nature, a time is reached that the human starting to differentiation and time is coming to reach again to Dead cell to Vibration.

What is Sarkar & Sanatan Sangha?

What is government?

1. The body is our first government. Which gives the way to live life.

2. Home is our second government. Which is the center of security, food, knowledge and health. Women is responsible for Home.

3. After the house, the third government is the temple of the locality which is the center of knowledge, health and all social works.

Currently the house is under break, and people doesn't have interest to move to street temple due to directionless politics.

No house should be destroyed, no temple should be left untouched so that politics of country should reach to complete.

For this purpose, various great men leave their dinner and even few are Lunch and meet almost all the saints and great men, go to the monastery and temple and bow down and receive knowledge from them regularly.

Everyone, just by donating one hour of time and one rupees in your street temples/Society, you will be healthy and will make others healthy and become rich.

The work of great men is to connect every school and hospital with the temple of that street,

Organizing Ayurveda seminars and workshops every day.

The temple will be so powerful that even those who do not have work will get work.

it is behaving like a center of justice.

Ayurveda is the Universe. Ayurveda is important in itself, which protects all the important points of common life.

Knowledge of this is necessary for all women so that ultimately deaths in the society should be reduced as Women can save to their husband, children and both parents.

For any patient this is necessary to control the vata, Pitta and Cough. This should be controlled by the following methods is as under -

VATA should be controlled by taking Triphala in night (monthly 3 day add Arandoil) . Take Pancharist, Dasmoolarist or Udaramrit in day time and ashokarishta specially for Women is the compulsory to avoid the PITTA dosha, if fever is there take fever medicine Jhandu Sudarshan Tablet or Amritaristm available on every ayurvedic shop. Self oil massage, Kumbhaka, Equalising of Respiration and watching of Respiration is three pranayam and gargling is compulsory to perform in morning, take the oil in nose, vapor bath or hot water bath weekly once or twice is essential to avoid the COUGH Dosha. Eating of one tea spoon Chyawanprash is a compulsory activity before breakfast and Avoid Dinner.

Week Women or Man can use daily in night Drasharisht . And for Cough and Cold Swaskoshsudha Pravahi Kwath should be taken and for any problem in respiration Arjunarist can be used.

DETOXIFICATION ACTIVITY (At every 6 months)

This is the activity of 14 days in home itself.

Daily Activity

1. Self - Oil Massage in Morning and Evening - 1 hrs.

2. Perform Kumbhaka pranayama, Equalising Respiration and watching the respiration for 30 minutes.

20 minute hot water bath or steam bath.

4. Nasya with medicated oil should be done in Morning and Evening time.

a) Kapha predominant - Use Cow ghee with Punarnava b) Pitta Predominant - Use Cow Ghee with Brahmi Ghee c) Vata predominant - Use Sesame Oil.

If unable to identify the Predominant then use Mustard oil itself.

5. Eat a khichdi mono diet with plenty of Ghee to oilation internally. Cold pressed flaxseed oil may be substituted in place of Ghee.

6. Perform Meditation from 1pm to 5. 30pm and 7pm to 9 pm.

7. Oil massage from 6pm to 7pm

8. Compulsory to take Triphala Tea at night. CCF tea (Cumin Coriander & Fennel) in the morning afternoon. Drink lots of warm water with squeezed lemon. Day 1 to 3 - Purvakarma Phase.

Day - 4 Eat a single clear diet as above. Drink coconut water, Rice congee etc.

In Evening take extra Triphala with 1 - 2 teaspoons of castor oil with warm water for better elimination.

Day - 5 Take plenty of 5 - 6 liters of warm water in the morning, and prepare for Basti.

If Bowel is not clear, perform enema with warm water to clean the Colon.

Further Dashmool/Sesame oil decoction and allow it for 20 minutes.

Take Rest 2 - 3 hrs.

Afternoon eat Khichdi. Drink plenty of warm water. Evening perform Meditation.

Day - 6 Perform Meditation Rest and Self - Care.

Eat Khichdi, take Ginger Tea.

Day - 7 to 14 Rasayana Day

1. Take Chyawanprash with warm water in Morning.
2. Drink Almond Date Milk and take normal food.

A CASE STUDY -

In Punaichak there is a four temple and one community center is running by the local people in which one in -

1. Devisthan Mohanpur
2. Devisthan Punnaichak village
3. Shiv mandir near Shashi Nandan Apartment and
4. Krishna Temple in Sabzi Mandi Punaichak.
5. Community Centre in Sabzi Mandi Punaichak.
6. Ram Lakhan High School, Punnaichak
7. Sri Jitendra Ji, sanghchalak of Rastriya Swayam Sevak Sangha

This all four Temple, School and Community center developed by the local people itself by collecting money from each other and helping each other to construct the temple. All the four temple have 4 different different pujari. Community center in Sabji Mandi have incharge and committee similarly school run by the committee and various teaching staff.

Devisthan Mohanpur is the oldest temple which never locked. Devotee mainly local women reaching the temple in morning and cleaning the temple in early morning and performing various puja of seven devi pind, hanuman, Lord Shiva, Ram Darbar, radhe Krishna, Pipal tree. Gathering women in temple in morning and singing various devotee song in joint and recording in mobile and publishing in U - tube channel. Whole day mainly women reaching to temple for puja and various other sanskar and activity in temple. In evening time also women are gathering and singing devotee song and recording and publishing in U - Tube channel. This temple was started under the pipal tree before 116 years as Mohanpur people was gathering under the peepal tree And gradually a temple was built. All the devotees or gossipers of Mohanpur used to come to this temple and used to gossip about what to do and what not to do and used to discuss it for the society. Gradually, A small temple was built, a priest came and started worshiping, bhajans started being sung in the morning and evening and in between some functions, big programs also started taking place. Wedding functions started, Mundan program started, naming of the child started. The program of children's Upanayanam Sanskar program has started. In this way, the temple has gradually completed its 116th year. Presently, the priest's son and great grandson are watching the puja. Mothers and sisters are doing the puja in the morning and evening. Nowadays, the political situation has become such that due to which less men come to the temples, but the women did not leave the temples, they took hold of the temples, there is morning and evening bhajan kirtan, whatever program there is, they come forward to participate in the work of Mohanpur society. It is a big thing that women are doing it and they are doing good work.

Devisthan Punnaichak village

Devi Sthan, which is situated in Punaichak village itself, was constructed more than 100 years ago. This temple was constructed by the people of the village 100 years ago when the people of the village did not have any temple, all the people were from home. They used to go out and used to sit at a cross roads where the temple is situated today and while sitting there, slowly and gradually a small temple was built. There people started performing their 16 rituals and today the temple has become very big, there is still a priest, his grandfather had started the puja there, today his father is doing it and it is a very good thing that here too, men are the first ones. People used to come more and in today's dates, women dominate. Be it Saturday, Monday or Tuesday, in the evening there is a fair of women and they keep singing songs of God.

Shiv mandir near Shashi Nandan Apartment

Shiv Temple which is next to Shashi Nandan Apartment, this temple was also prepared after the local meeting here and this temple is very small but the priests here work very hard to open the temple at 5:00 in the morning and close at 9:00 in the night. Be it Tuesday or Saturday, Monday, the gathering of women does not decrease when women come here, sing many songs, do bhajans and keep the temple awake. The temple has become a big center for 16 rituals. Today's Dates There are no people of this area who are left out of this temple because many scholars keep coming to temple who are masters of 16 rituals and help in it, this is a big thing.

4. Krishna Temple in Sabzi Mandi Punaichak.

There is a very big temple next to the vegetable market in the market of Punaichak. It is famous for the name of Krishna Temple. It is a very magnificent temple. This is also a temple built by the village of Punaichak, where there is a photo of Lord Krishna and Radha and an idol is also installed. There is a lot of bhajan and kirtan happening here. People in the market worship here with great heart. Many people from outside come and perform programs here. 16 rituals are performed in this temple for seven consecutive days. It is a very good temple.

5. Community Centre in Sabzi Mandi Punaichak.

There is a community center in the market itself which is very important, be it someone's wedding, any big function or any kind of program in this area, whatever happens in this area happens here, it is also built by local people and run by them. There is a very good system for preparing food and drinks and also for taking it forward.

6. Ram Lakhan High School, Punnaichak

There is a very good school in Punaichak, Ram Lakhan High School, it provides education up to 10 + 2. This school is also on the land of Punaichak, it was built by them and the children grow there. Today, the government even hires its own staff and runs it.

7. CASE OF SRI JITENDRA JI, Sanghchalak Rastriya Swam Sevak Sangha.

Sri Jitendra ji is the Ist 40 year old Sanghi. There is a temple of Lord Shiva above his house, he gets up daily at 2:00am in the night and has been serving Lord Shiva in the temple for 40 years non - stop. His day is very wonderful. 2:00 am 3am or Three to four get ready and performing puja till 4:30am, then after 4:30am, have some tea and go out to the field. They go to the Sangh's park shakha, where he set up park shakha and exercises there.

We do yoga together plus do some talks also, then he discusses how the program continues daily from 9am to 10am in the day, then they come home, have food and drinks, ask the children to leave the child to study, then the child returns in the evening. He goes to bring him and perform the evening puja very loudly at his home, then he has many friends like politicians, meet him and be friend him and then he wants all his people to talk once to take blessings, this is Baba's Jitendra.

Sri Jitendra ji is not taking dinner last few year.

In patna most of the street and temple known to him.

Hindu society is a union where three governments function, first of yourself, second of your home and third of the monastery and temple of your locality.

If there is any social work, only the local Math and Temple is useful.

Only the people of the locality come to work. The one who protects from the heart is a Kshatriya, the one who has acquired knowledge is a knowledgeable person, the one who does business is a businessman and the one who serves is a Shudra.

In this, one who is born in a Brahmin family is the best, the one born in a Brahmin family is the best, the Kshatriya family and the family doing Kshatriya work is the best, the Vaishya family and the family doing Vaishya work is the Vaishya best, the one born in the Shudra family is the Shudra. Is the best.

Marriages and relationships connect us, two families and two villages.

The workers of the local temple together form the Gram Panchayat or Community Committee, the workers of the Gram Panchayat or community from the District Committee, the workers of the District Committee together form the State Committee and the State Committee forms the Country Committee.

The incharge of this committee is the head, the district president, the collector, the chief minister, the governor and the prime minister the president.

Gram Panchayat or committee Math Temple is to be with the Panchayat House, District level Math Temple is to be with the Collector Bhawan, State level Math Temple is to be with the Governor Bhawan and Country level Math Temple is to be with the Rashtrapati Bhavan.

Other places like House, Parliament, School, College, Court, Jail etc. are for the protection and good of our and our temple.

It is necessary to build a permanent monastery/Math and temple of Shankaracharya along with the President house with Math and Mandir with minimum seat of 10000 next to the Parliament and Assembly buildings.

It is necessary to have a temporary residence of Shankaracharya here on a rotational basis.

Political Party is a product from the Street temple Karyakarta starting from Street Temple to other village in marriage and relation activity it further creating Gram or Community Panchayat to District Panchayat to State Panchayat to Country Panchayat to World Panchayat itself.

Political party developing from the state level to country level.

In india political party is forming without any acharya in that political party office, hence they are some time talking and doing in right direction and some time moving in wrong direction due to improper discipline and personal ego etc.

It is necessary to build a permanent monastery or math and temple for the representative of Shankaracharya next to the Collector, Assistant Collector and Gram Panchayat Community buildings.

It is necessary to have a temporary residence of the representative of Shankaracharya here on a rotational basis.

Both cow and bull give us oxygen 24x7, hence their protection is life, hence cow and bull slaughter should be stopped, sale of cow meat should be banned with immediate effect.

The bull will automatically become a part of the economy. This is the responsibility of every individual in country to think over and act accordingly.

If bull slaughtering is not stopped then man will also be slaughtered and only the Chief Minister of the state and the Prime Minister of the country are responsible for it.

Twenty Four Hour Sangha

Our body itself is the twenty Four hour Sangha, which is a self powerful. No one can control the human being.

Every Human being is unique and itself controlling self.

The body is an entity that creates and controls itself no matter what the situation may be. Now see, when the body is inside the mother's womb, it neither takes any food nor breathes nor drinks water. Neither does it get sunlight, but inside the stomach also, the body grows by two and a half kilos due to one vibration and when the child comes out of the mother's womb, he does not breathe. After coming to the earth, his breathing starts. Now see, inside the stomach they are connected to the mother's navel, they keep getting energy from it and they remain alive, they make adjustments only in the mother's stomach, which develop their body with energy and when they come out, they breathe. Let's start with the meaning of breath, which is connected to nature like the navel and integrate it into our body, then we also fear, in this way there is another part of the body, there is the mind, other lessons which are connected to this nature. Let's go to this very big science, no man or any living being can run their life, it is their own, not inside the womb, that is, from the mother's citizen, their body was running, that is, till death or as long as it is in nature, it is theirs. The connection with the mother remains after coming to earth, they get connected with the environment and as long as there is breath, that is, as long as they are connected to the nature, the breathing continues and they are connected to the nature, the mind is connected, all the information is connected. Therefore, the body itself does all the work 24/7 or as long as it is alive, it will not run only with breathing, breathing is going on, mind is working, hands and legs are working. Only then this life continues.

Human being is attached with the mother and once reaching to earth attaching with the Environment. Vibration and formation of dead cell have connection with the Universe. If Human or any creatures who is following the Law of nature, Climate and Environment is always helped by the Nature, Climate and Environment.

Twelve Hour Sangha

Be it family business or any work which is done permanently for development in a coordinated manner, it is a 12 - hour union, it is a family, people work outside and come to the family in the evening and then are in the family from evening till morning. On top of that, there is a latrine in the middle, there is sleeping in the bathroom, what kind of union is this, we can call it a 12 hour union.

One Hour Sangha

Now see, we went to the temple, sat there for an hour, some do meditation, some talk next to them, some read Geeta, some read Ramayana, some are reciting Hanuman Chalisa, some are doing puja and some people sit in the courtyard of the temple and socialize. We are discussing about, we are planning something different, we are planning to make something, so what is this, we go out of the house for an hour, sit for an hour and do some meditation, those who go and come do this, this is the Sangh, those who talk in it This association is called One Hour Association, this association is also formed at our intersection, people are drinking tea at the intersection, then there is a shop next to it, they are gossiping that this should be there in this area and there that. It should be like this, it is not happening, it is not happening, it should be like this, this government is bad, this government should be like this, I should become a minister, I should become this, so and so's son, this is her daughter, this is her marriage, she is not getting married.

This is how discussions go on at the intersections, at tea shops, at barber shops for cutting hair and many other things on that. While discussing when development will happen, is that place there a little If you give it, we will set up a shop, then someone gives even a little space and if the shop is set up, then one hour's association leads to another, that is why it is said that one hour's association which runs the country is 12 hours' association. The union through which the family runs, the business runs and the 24 - hour union which is to run oneself.

We can take many examples on this. Now see, now there are 200 or 400 people in a park, some are roaming, some are doing yoga, some are meditating. Someone is chatting, someone is doing something, someone is doing something, in this way they keep doing something or the other, and how many days they stay there, did some exercise, did something wrong, made some friendship, talked about their children, about something In the discussions going on about the government, about the country, about the foreign country, some program has taken place, a program of party has taken place or a program of some other party has taken place, someone is writing a book, his program has taken place, someone else has made a project. Its program was done, in this way the park would have become as Bollywood as it is, people were going to visit the park here, but the law of the entire country is being made, the law of the entire society is being made, it is a big thing, take more like this.

Like people go to take bath in the Ganga, let's say it is a full moon day, Amavasya or any other special day, there also people can give the same amount and worship, there should be development of Ganga, this should happen here, this should happen there, that should happen. In the same way, many examples can be taken, which of us, now see, we are people, we live at home, build houses, now the whole world cannot run from home, so we leave the house, where will we go, we have gathered at one place, but we have gathered.

Brother, when did we do something, this is our problem, we have this problem, he has this problem, the other person's problem is that while talking to him, we slowly turn it into a temple, some priest also sits in the temple and starts worshiping in the temple, then the same again. Over time, along with the temple, the place also becomes a center of business, someone is selling flowers, someone is selling books, someone is studying there, someone is studying, a shop is opened, a school is opened, a hospital is opened, it is from the temples. It hardly takes one hour to fulfill our needs, so think how important is the time of one hour, our society is built by it and all the necessary things in the society are fulfilled from there, especially the 16 sanskars which are All that is required is given in one hour only.

How Math Mandir Formed

What happens when a program of 1 hour starts and people meet at one place, then this decision is gradually taken from the program of meeting, why don't we create such a place where we meet daily and chat so that the solution to our problem becomes the best for them? Well, either we sit under a tree or take a room in someone's house and chat there and some people come out and say why don't we build a temple there and we will worship there. When will you sit and do it? Gradually, a small temple is built there and we start worshiping there. When does it start happening? How can our security in this area be better? We live here for the good in that too. We mean the force.

If you think, the force is also formed from there, brother, it is okay, for our security, three - four men will stay awake at night and provide security, they will use sticks without driving, they learn exercise, do yoga so that they remain fit, then there is something in the same to see our children. People also start teaching so that the children start imparting values to good people so that more children become good and things get better in the future. A school is formed and a small hospital is also built there. Ayurvedic center, health center, health center. Where someone gathers for a dispute, Panchakarma is done for the benefit of his health, some Ayurvedic activity is done, in the village at night in the locality, if there is no one there, then if someone says that he knows whether he is a relative or not. We stay in their house, otherwise what is there, some temple is built, there is a school in it, education is also being done, accommodation arrangements are made, food arrangements are made there, one can stay there. If we can eat, we can worship in the temple, the monastery, temple, school, hospital gets built automatically and the center of our protector gets ready from there, the business gets ready automatically.

A CASE STUDY OF 16 SANSKAR -

What is SANATAN PARAMPARA (HINDUISM) & DISCIPLINE

SANATAN have the option to follow all chapters of GITA from 1 to 18 from Birth to Death in different different stages. Sanatan people follow the 16 Sanskar, which comes in different phases of life which includes the 18 chapter of GITA.

There are Nine works divided which indicate to perform any work with devotion, that work will give peace to the concerned People.

Sacred Sixteen Sacraments of Hinduism (SANATAN)

Hinduism (Sanatan) is the theme of India. In this, sixteen sacred rites are performed.

Due to the antiquity and vastness of Hinduism, it is also called 'Sanatan Dharma' as every quality developed due to various natural reasons.

SANATAN (Hinduism) , like Buddhism, Jainism, Christianity, Islam, etc. , is not a Community established by any particular person, but a large set of different communities and beliefs that have been going on since ancient times.

According to Maharishi Ved Vyas, sixteen sacred sacraments are performed from birth to death for betterment and safety of life.

Which is as follows : -

(1) . Conception ceremony, (2) . Punsavan rituals. (3) . Seemantonnayan Sanskar, (4) . Jatkarma Sanskar, (5) . Naming Ceremony,

(6) . The evacuation ceremony, (7) . Annaprashan Sanskar, (8) Chudakarma Sanskar, (9) . Vidyarambha Sanskar, (10. Karnavedha Sanskar, (11) . Yagyopaveet Sanskar, (12) . Vedarambh Sanskar, (13) . Keshant Sanskar, (14) . Samvartan Sanskar, (15) . Marriage & Economic rites, (16) . Funeral rites.

1. Garbhadhana - samskara (Conception) : Maharishi Charak has said that it is necessary for pregnancy to be happy and strong in the mind, that is why men and women should always eat the right food and remain happy always.

At the time of conception, the mind of man and woman should be filled with enthusiasm, happiness and health.

In order to get a good child, first of all, conception - sanskar has to be done.

Pregnancy is produced by the combination of Raj and Semen of the parents. This coincidence is called conception.

The physical union of a man and a woman is called garbhadhana - samskara a very natural samaskara.

After pregnancy, there are attacks of many types of natural defects, to avoid which this sanskar is performed.

By which the pregnancy remains safe.

Good and suitable progeny are produced from the insemination done with proper rituals.

An Ayurvedic Hospital at Village level is essential to help the every individual for the above Sanskar.

Women getting period in 28 days of cycle from Moon. This is of 3 days and women becoming normal in 5 - 7 days.

If Man will create vibration to women then the product should be as under -

What is the method to perform this ritual?

Sankalpa (Resolve) : The man should recite the mantra which says, 'I am performing the samskara of Garbhadhana to be blessed with an excellent progeny and to destroy the inhibitions in my sperms and her ovum and those in her womb as well. '

अस्याः मम भार्यायाः तिगर्भ संस्कारातिशय द्वारा अस्यां जनिष्यमाण-
सर्वगर्भाणां बीजगर्भ समुद्भवैनो निबर्हणद्वारा श्री परमेश्वर प्रीत्यर्थं गर्भाधानाख्यं कर्म
करिष्ये ।

Pradhanajyahoma: It is a small yagna where the couple offers oblation to Lord Vishnu and deity Prajapati by reciting mantras. Then, put 3 - 4 drops of Druva juice into the right nostril of the woman. After reciting the below mantra, bow to the sun, deities and elders in the family. Have a meal after this, wear a new dress and decorate the room. The man should place his hand on the woman's navel and begin this samskara.

Upasthasparsha Mantra

ॐ गन्धर्वस्य विश्वावसोर्मुखमसि ।
ॐ विष्णुर्योनिं कल्पयतु त्वष्टा रूपाणि पिंशतु ।
आ सिञ्चतु जापतिर्धाता गर्भं दधातु ते ॥
ॐ गर्भं धेहि सिनीवालि गर्भं धेहि सरस्वति ।
गर्भं ते अश्विनौ देवावा धत्तां पुष्करदाजा ॥
ॐ हिरण्ययी अरणीयं निर्मन्थतो अश्विना ।
तं ते गर्भं हवामहे दशमे मासि सूतवे ॥

This sloka says: 'Oh woman, you are the mouth of Vishwavasu Gandharva and may Lord Vishnu make this your birth passage useful for Garbhadhana. May Tvashta heal your organs. May Prajapati make the semen fertile and Dhata make it useful for conceiving. O' Deity Siniwali, please protect this foetus and Lord Saraswati, please help the process of conceiving. Ashwin Kumar, who holds the golden lotus, may stabilize the foetus and establish the foetus within 10 months. '

Favorable time & nakshatras for this ritual

4th and 16th lunar days after menstruation.

6th, 8th, 9th, 10th, 12th, 14th full moon and new moon days are also auspicious. Favourable nakshatras are Uttaraphalguni, Uttarashada, Uttarabadrapadh, Rohini, Mrigashira, Anuradha, Hasta, Swati, Shravan, Dhanishta, and Satabhisha.

This act should be done by the couple in a cheerful and happy state of mind. Do not indulge in sex during the menstrual cycles.

This samskara is done after marriage, from the 5th to the 16th day after the 1st menses. Excluding the 1st, 4th, 11th, and 13th nights, the other ten nights are considered appropriate to perform this samskara.

Here are the magic numbers. Male Child: Days 6, 8, 10, 12, 14 & 16 from commencement of menstruation. Female Child: Days 5, 7, 9, & 15 from the commencement of menstruation. No other days are good for conception and there are a few blackout days as well depending on the phase of the moon.

2. Punsavan: : Punsavan Sanskar is organized after three months because the brain of the fetus starts developing after three months in the womb.

At this time, the foundation of the sanskars of the child born in the womb is laid through the Punsavan Sanskar.

The child starts learning in the womb, an example of this is Abhimanyu who had received the education of Chakravyuha in the womb of mother Subhdra.

What is done in Punsavan Sanskar?

As per one ritual, a paste is prepared mixing yoghurt, milk and ghee (clarified butter) , by the husband himself, and he then feeds it to his wife. As per another, which would be a more elaborate one than this, the ritual is performed in the presence of the Yajna Fire and while chanting Vedic Chants and Hymns.

Smell of Giloe ras to be taken by pregnant Women.

औषधि अवघ्राण के लिए वट वृक्ष की जटाओं के मुलायम सिरों का छोटा टुकड़ा, गिलोय, पीपल की कोंपल (मुलायम पत्ते) लाकर रखे जाएँ। सबका थोड़ा - थोड़ा अंश पानी के साथ सिल पर पीसकर एक कटोरी में उसका घोल तैयार रखा जाए। 2 साबूदाने या चावल की खीर तैयार रखी जाए।

This is the responsibility of every society to develop the Social health centre where Pregnant ladies can get help to develop.

2. पुंसवन संस्कार

3. Seemantonnayan - Seemantonnayan Sanskar is performed in the fourth, sixth and eighth months of pregnancy.

At this time the child growing in the womb becomes capable of learning.

To bring knowledge of good qualities, nature and deeds, the mother has to behave in the right way. .

During this, the mother should study by staying calm and happy.

सीमन्तोन्नयन का अभिप्राय है सौभाग्य संपन्न होना। गर्भपात रोकने के साथ - साथ गर्भस्थ शिशु एवं उसकी माता की रक्षा करना भी इस संस्कार का मुख्य उद्देश्य है। इस संस्कार के माध्यम से गर्भिणी स्त्री का मन प्रसन्न रखने के लिये पति गर्भवती की मांग भरता हैं। यह संस्कार गर्भ धारण के छठे अथवा आठवें महीने में होता है।

3. सीमन्तोनयन संस्कार

4. Jatakram: By performing Jatkarma Sanskar as soon as the child is born, many types of defects of the child are removed.

When Child takes birth at that time the child is not taking any breadth and in a few seconds the child starts to take breadth and the family enjoys that occasions.

Under this, on the sixth day the baby is licked with honey and ghee, as well as Vedic mantras are recited so that the child is healthy and long.

On the basis of Jyotish Science Jatakarma is performed for a born child, this Sanskar helps families to train the Child in the same field for better development and benefit to the Society.

In the Present World, mostly children take birth in hospitals, hence the Hospital and their mother father know the Date of Birth, hence this is the responsibility of all Parents and Street temple to train the human being as per their quality.

Now the question arises, what should be the type of human being?

There are four qualities of human beings as Brahmin, Kshtriya, Vaishya and Shudra.

The Land is also of four similar qualities, Nature also has four similar qualities.

Quality	Brahmin	Kshatriya	Vaishya	Shudra
Land	Brahmin (White Soil)	Kshatriya (Hilly Area)	Vaishya (Mix Soil)	Shudra (Black Soil)
Nature	Brahmin (12AM to 6 AM) & 4PM	Kshatriya (6AM to 12 PM)	Vaishya (12 PM to 4 PM)	Shudra (6PM to 12AM)

	to 6PM)			
Human Being	Brahmin (Thinker and who is working for Country)	Kshatriya (Force, Army)	Vaishya (Businessm an)	Shudra (Serving to anyone)
Human Being & Work	Brahmin (Teaching, Research) Income from accepting DAN.	Kshatriya (Safety) Income from accepting Taxes.	Vaishya (Business) Income from Profit.	Shudra (Helping others) Income from Salary.

Types of Human being is as under -

Place of Birth and nature is the primary concern.

Example any children born in Ganga or Gandak region where its soil is white is of Brahmin is always a powerful tool which Creates major quality in children whether they are born as a brahmin, Kshtriya , Vaishya and Shudra.

Nature is another important feature which changes the quality of children. Suppose any child born in the morning 2. 30am to 6am before sunrise, will get the quality of Brahmin.

Similarly following quality is as under -

1. Brahmin - Brahmin - Brahmin - Brahmin
2. Brahmin - Brahmin - Brahmin - Kshtriya
3. Brahmin - Brahmin - Brahmin - Vaishya
4. Brahmin - Brahmin - Brahmin - Shudra
5. Brahmin - Brahmin - Kshtriya - Brahmin
6. Brahmin - Brahmin - vaishya - Brahmin
7. Brahmin - Brahman - Shudra - Brahmin

8. Brahmin - Brahmin - Kshtriya - Kshtriya
9. Brahmin - Brahmin - Vaishya - Kshtriya
10. Brahmin - Brahmin - Shudra - Kshtriya
11. Brahmin - Brahmin - Kshtriya - Vaishya
12. Brahmin - Brahmin - Vaishya - Vaishya
13. Brahmin - Brahmin - Shudra - Vaishya
14. Brahmin - Brahmin - Kshtriya - Shudra
15. Brahmin - Brahmin - Vaishya - Shudra
16. Brahmin - Brahmin - Shudra - Shudra
17. Brahmin - Kshtriya - Brahmin - Brahmin
18. Brahmin - Kshtriya - Brahmin - Kshtriya
19. Brahmin - Kshtriya - Brahmin - Vaishya
20. Brahmin - Kshtriya - Brahmin - Shudra
21. Brahmin - Kshtriya - Kshtriya - Brahmin
22. Brahmin - Kshtriya - Kshtriya - Kshtriya
23. Brahmin - Kshtriya - Kshtriya - Vaishya
24. Brahmin - Kshtriya - Kshtriya - Shudra
25. Brahmin - Kshtriya - Vaishya - Brahmin
26. Brahmin - Kshtriya - Vaishya - Kshtriya
27. Brahmin - Kshtriya - Vaishya - Vaishya
28. Brahmin - Kshtriya - Vaishya - Shudra
29. Brahmin - Kshtriya - Shudra - Brahmin
30. Brahmin - Kshtriya - Shudra - Kshtriya
31. Brahmin - Kshtriya - Shudra - Vaishya
32. Brahmin - Kshtriya - Shudra - Shudra
33. Brahmin - Vaishya - Brahmin - Brahmin

34. Brahmin - Vaishya - Brahmin - Kshtriya
35. Brahmin - Vaishya - Brahmin - Vaishya
36. Brahmin - Vaishya - Brahmin - Shudra
37. Brahmin - Vaishya - Kshtriya - Brahmin
38. Brahmin - Vaishya - Kshtriya - Kshtriya
39. Brahmin - Vaishya - Kshtriya - Vaishya
40. Brahmin - Vaishya - Kshtriya - Shudra
41. Brahmin - Vaishya - Vaishya - Brahmin
42. Brahmin - Vaishya - Vaishya - Kshtriya
43. Brahmin - Vaishya - Vaishya - Vaishya
44. Brahmin - Vaishya - Vaishya - Shudra
45. Brahmin - Vaishya - Shudra - Brahmin
46. Brahmin - Vaishya - Shudra - Kshtriya
47. Brahmin - Vaishya - Shudra - Vaishya
48. Brahmin - Vaishya - Shudra - Shudra
49. Brahmin - Shudra - Brahmin - Brahmin
50. Brahmin - Shudra - Brahmin - Kshtriya
51. Brahmin - Shudra - Brahmin - Vaishya
52. Brahmin - Shudra - Brahmin - Shudra
53. Brahmin - Shudra - Kshtriya - Brahmin
54. Brahmin - Shudra - Kshtriya - Kshtriya
55. Brahmin - Shudra - Kshtriya - Vaishya
56. Brahmin - Shudra - Kshtriya - Shudra
57. Brahmin - Shudra - Vaishya - Brahmin
58. Brahmin - Shudra - Vaishya - Kshtriya
59. Brahmin - Shudra - Vaishya - Vaishya

60. Brahmin - Shudra - Vaishya - Shudra
61. Brahmin - Shudra - Shudra - Brahmin
62. Brahmin - Shudra - Shudra - Kshtriya
63. Brahmin - Shudra - Shudra - Vaishya
64. Brahmin - Shudra - Shudra - Shudra
65. Kshtriya - Brahmin - Brahmin - Brahmin
66. Kshtriya - Brahmin - Brahmin - Kshtriya
67. Kshtriya - Brahmin - Brahmin - Vaishya
68. Kshtriya - Brahmin - Brahmin - Shudra
69. Kshtriya - Brahmin - Kshtriya - Brahmin
70. Kshtriya - Brahmin - vaishya - Brahmin
71. Kshatriya - Brahmin - Shudra - Brahmin
72. Kshtriya - Brahmin - Kshtriya - Kshtriya
73. Kshtriya - Brahmin - Vaishya - Kshtriya
74. Kshtriya - Brahmin - Shudra - Kshtriya
75. Kshtriya - Brahmin - Kshtriya - Vaishya
76. Kshtriya - Brahmin - Vaishya - Vaishya
77. Kshtriya - Brahmin - Shudra - Vaishya
78. Kshtriya - Brahmin - Kshtriya - Shudra
79. Kshtriya - Brahmin - Vaishya - Shudra
80. Kshtriya - Brahmin - Shudra - Shudra
81. Kshtriya - Kshtriya - Brahmin - Brahmin
82. Kshtriya - Kshtriya - Brahmin - Kshtriya
83. Kshtriya - Kshtriya - Brahmin - Vaishya
84. Kshtriya - Kshtriya - Brahmin - Shudra
85. Kshtriya - Kshtriya - Kshtriya - Brahmin

86. Kshtriya - Kshtriya - Kshtriya - Kshtriya
87. Kshtriya - Kshtriya - Kshtriya - Vaishya
88. Kshtriya - Kshtriya - Kshtriya - Shudra
89. Kshtriya - Kshtriya - Vaishya - Brahmin
90. Kshtriya - Kshtriya - Vaishya - Kshtriya
91. Kshtriya - Kshtriya - Vaishya - Vaishya
92. Kshtriya - Kshtriya - Vaishya - Shudra
93. Kshtriya - Kshtriya - Shudra - Brahmin
94. Kshtriya - Kshtriya - Shudra - Kshtriya
95. Kshtriya - Kshtriya - Shudra - Vaishya
96. Kshtriya - Kshtriya - Shudra - Shudra
97. Kshtriya - Vaishya - Brahmin - Brahmin
98. Kshtriya - Vaishya - Brahmin - Kshtriya
99. Kshtriya - Vaishya - Brahmin - Vaishya
100. Kshtriya - Vaishya - Brahmin - Shudra
101. Kshtriya - Vaishya - Kshtriya - Brahmin
102. Kshtriya - Vaishya - Kshtriya - Kshtriya
103. Kshtriya - Vaishya - Kshtriya - Vaishya
104. Kshtriya - Vaishya - Kshtriya - Shudra
105. Kshtriya - Vaishya - Vaishya - Brahmin
106. Kshtriya - Vaishya - Vaishya - Kshtriya
107. Kshtriya - Vaishya - Vaishya - Vaishya
108. Kshtriya - Vaishya - Vaishya - Shudra
109. Kshtriya - Vaishya - Shudra - Brahmin
110. Kshtriya - Vaishya - Shudra - Kshtriya
111. Kshtriya - Vaishya - Shudra - Vaishya

112. Kshtriya - Vaishya - Shudra - Shudra
113. Kshtriya - Shudra - Brahmin - Brahmin
114. Kshtriya - Shudra - Brahmin - Kshtriya
115. Kshtriya - Shudra - Brahmin - Vaishya
116. Kshtriya - Shudra - Brahmin - Shudra
117. Kshtriya - Shudra - Kshtriya - Brahmin
118. Kshtriya - Shudra - Kshtriya - Kshtriya
119. Kshtriya - Shudra - Kshtriya - Vaishya
120. Kshtriya - Shudra - Kshtriya - Shudra
121. Kshtriya - Shudra - Vaishya - Brahmin
122. Kshtriya - Shudra - Vaishya - Kshtriya
123. Kshtriya - Shudra - Vaishya - Vaishya
124. Kshtriya - Shudra - Vaishya - Shudra
125. Kshtriya - Shudra - Shudra - Brahmin
126. Kshtriya - Shudra - Shudra - Kshtriya
127. Kshtriya - Shudra - Shudra - Vaishya
128. Kshatriya - Shudra - Shudra - Shudra
129. Vaishya - Brahmin - Brahmin - Brahmin
130. Vaishya - Brahmin - Brahmin - Kshtriya
131. Vaishya - Brahmin - Brahmin - Vaishya
132. Vaishya - Brahmin - Brahmin - Shudra
133. Vaishya - Brahmin - Kshtriya - Brahmin
134. Vaishya - Brahmin - vaishya - Brahmin
135. Vaishya - Brahman - Shudra - Brahmin
136. Vaishya - Brahmin - Kshtriya - Kshtriya
137. Vaishya - Brahmin - Vaishya - Kshtriya

138. Vaishya - Brahmin - Shudra - Kshtriya
139. Vaishya - Brahmin - Kshtriya - Vaishya
140. Vaishya - Brahmin - Vaishya - Vaishya
141. Vaishya - Brahmin - Shudra - Vaishya
142. Vaishya - Brahmin - Kshtriya - Shudra
143. Vaishya - Brahmin - Vaishya - Shudra
144. Vaishya - Brahmin - Shudra - Shudra
145. Vaishya - Kshtriya - Brahmin - Brahmin
146. Vaishya - Kshtriya - Brahmin - Kshtriya
147. Vaishya - Kshtriya - Brahmin - Vaishya
148. Vaishya - Kshatriya - Brahmin - Shudra
149. Vaishya - Kshtriya - Kshtriya - Brahmin
150. Vaishya - Kshtriya - Kshtriya - Kshtriya
151. Vaishya - Kshtriya - Kshtriya - Vaishya
152. Vaishya - Kshtriya - Kshtriya - Shudra
153. Vaishya - Kshtriya - Vaishya - Brahmin
154. Vaishya - Kshtriya - Vaishya - Kshtriya
155. Vaishya - Kshtriya - Vaishya - Vaishya
156. Vaishya - Kshtriya - Vaishya - Shudra
157. Vaishya - Kshtriya - Shudra - Brahmin
158. Vaishya - Kshtriya - Shudra - Kshtriya
159. Vaishya - Kshtriya - Shudra - Vaishya
160. Vaishya - Kshtriya - Shudra - Shudra
161. Vaishya - Vaishya - Brahmin - Brahmin
162. Vaishya - Vaishya - Brahmin - Kshtriya
163. Vaishya - Vaishya - Brahmin - Vaishya

164. Vaishya - Vaishya - Brahmin - Shudra
165. Vaishya - Vaishya - Kshtriya - Brahmin
166. Vaishya - Vaishya - Kshtriya - Kshtriya
167. Vaishya - Vaishya - Kshtriya - Vaishya
168. Vaishya - Vaishya - Kshtriya - Shudra
169. Vaishya - Vaishya - Vaishya - Brahmin
170. Vaishya - Vaishya - Vaishya - Kshtriya
171. Vaishya - Vaishya - Vaishya - Vaishya
172. Vaishya - Vaishya - Vaishya - Shudra
173. Vaishya - Vaishya - Shudra - Brahmin
174. Vaishya - Vaishya - Shudra - Kshtriya
175. Vaishya - Vaishya - Shudra - Vaishya
176. Vaishya - Vaishya - Shudra - Shudra
177. Vaishya - Shudra - Brahmin - Brahmin
178. Vaishya - Shudra - Brahmin - Kshtriya
179. Vaishya - Shudra - Brahmin - Vaishya
180. Vaishya - Shudra - Brahmin - Shudra
181. Vaishya - Shudra - Kshtriya - Brahmin
182. Vaishya - Shudra - Kshtriya - Kshtriya
183. Vaishya - Shudra - Kshtriya - Vaishya
184. Vaishya - Shudra - Kshtriya - Shudra
185. Vaishy - Shudra - Vaishya - Brahmin
186. Vaishya - Shudra - Vaishya - Kshtriya
187. Vaishya - Shudra - Vaishya - Vaishya
188. Vaishya - Shudra - Vaishya - Shudra
189. Vaishya - Shudra - Shudra - Brahmin

190. Vaishya - Shudra - Shudra - Kshtriya
191. Vaishya - Shudra - Shudra - Vaishya
192. Vaishya - Shudra - Shudra - Shudra
193. Shudra - Brahmin - Brahmin - Brahmin
194. Shudra - Brahmin - Brahmin - Kshtriya
195. Shudra - Brahmin - Brahmin - Vaishya
196. Shudra - Brahmin - Brahmin - Shudra
197. Shudra - Brahmin - Kshtriya - Brahmin
198. Shudra - Brahmin - vaishya - Brahmin
199. Shudra - Brahman - Shudra - Brahmin
200. Shudra - Brahmin - Kshtriya - Kshtriya
201. Shudra - Brahmin - Vaishya - Kshtriya
202. Shudra - Brahmin - Shudra - Kshtriya
203. Shudra - Brahmin - Kshtriya - Vaishya
204. Shudra - Brahmin - Vaishya - Vaishya
205. Shudra - Brahmin - Shudra - Vaishya
206. Shudra - Brahmin - Kshatriya - Shudra
207. Shudra - Brahmin - Vaishya - Shudra
208. Shudra - Brahmin - Shudra - Shudra
209. Shudra - Kshtriya - Brahmin - Brahmin
210. Shudra - Kshtriya - Brahmin - Kshtriya
211. Shudra - Kshtriya - Brahmin - Vaishya
212. Shudra - Kshtriya - Brahmin - Shudra
213. Shudra - Kshtriya - Kshtriya - Brahmin
214. Shudra - Kshtriya - Kshtriya - Kshtriya
215. Shudra - Kshtriya - Kshtriya - Vaishya

216. Shudra - Kshtriya - Kshtriya - Shudra
217. Shudra - Kshtriya - Vaishya - Brahmin
218. Shudra - Kshtriya - Vaishya - Kshtriya
219. Shudra - Kshtriya - Vaishya - Vaishya
220. Shudra - Kshtriya - Vaishya - Shudra
221. Shudra - Kshtriya - Shudra - Brahmin
222. Shudra - Kshtriya - Shudra - Kshtriya
223. Shudra - Kshtriya - Shudra - Vaishya
224. Shudra - Kshatriya - Shudra - Shudra
225. Shudra - Vaishya - Brahmin - Brahmin
226. Shudra - Vaishya - Brahmin - Kshtriya
227. Shudra - Vaishya - Brahmin - Vaishya
228. Shudra - Vaishya - Brahmin - Shudra
229. Shudra - Vaishya - Kshtriya - Brahmin
230. Shudra - Vaishya - Kshtriya - Kshtriya
231. Shudra - Vaishya - Kshtriya - Vaishya
232. Shudra - Vaishya - Kshtriya - Shudra
233. Shudr - Vaishya - Vaishya - Brahmin
234. Shudra - Vaishya - Vaishya - Kshtriya
235. Shudr - Vaishya - Vaishya - Vaishya
236. Shudra - Vaishya - Vaishya - Shudra
237. Shudra - Vaishya - Shudra - Brahmin
238. Shudra - Vaishya - Shudra - Kshtriya
239. Shudra - Vaishya - Shudra - Vaishya
240. Shudr - Vaishya - Shudra - Shudra
241. Shudra - Shudra - Brahmin - Brahmin

242. Shudra - Shudra - Brahmin - Kshtriya
243. Shudra - Shudra - Brahmin - Vaishya
244. Shudra - Shudra - Brahmin - Shudra
245. Shudra - Shudra - Kshtriya - Brahmin
246. Shudra - Shudra - Kshtriya - Kshtriya
247. Shudra - Shudra - Kshtriya - Vaishya
248. Shudra - Shudra - Kshatriya - Shudra
249. Shudra - Shudra - Vaishya - Brahmin
250. Shudra - Shudra - Vaishya - Kshtriya
251. Shudra - Shudra - Vaishya - Vaishya
252. Shudra - Shudra - Vaishya - Shudra
253. Shudra - Shudra - Shudra - Brahmin
254. Shudra - Shudra - Shudra - Kshatriya
255. Shudra - Shudra - Shudra - Vaishya
256. Shudra - Shudra - Shudra - Shudra

Various combinations giving various qualities of Children or human beings, needs training as essential similar to Quality comes in Astrology Report.

Thirty two qualities of children taking birth in any specific place depends on time of birth and quality.

Sixty four qualities of children taking birth in any specific place depends on their time of birth, parents' quality and their parents' business.

Sometimes places quality also differing in that case in one area 256 types of children will take birth.

This is the activity of society and Street temple to develop the 256 technology and as per suitability of area to be taught to the Children in

Schooling till 17th of age.

4. जातकर्म संस्कार

5. Naamkaran: -

After the Jatkarma, the naming ceremony is performed.

On the basis of Jyotis , name suggests, the name of the child is kept in it.

The naming ceremony is performed on the 11th day after the birth of the child.

The name of the child is decided according to astrology. Many people name their child whatever is wrong.

It affects his mindset and his future.

Just as wearing good clothes enhances the personality, similarly having a good and concise name has its effect on the whole life.

The thing to keep in mind is that the name of the child should be kept in such a way that he is called or known by that name at home and outside.

5. नामकरण संस्कार

6. Nishkraman: -

After this, the Nishkraman ceremony is performed in the fourth month of birth.

The meaning of expulsion is to take out.

Our body is made up of earth, water, fire, air and sky etc. which are called Panchabhutas.

Therefore the father prays to these deities for the welfare of the child.

Also wish the baby a long life and a healthy life.

6. निष्क्रमण संस्कार

7. Annaprashan: Annaprashan Sanskar is performed at the time of teething of the child i. e. at the age of 6 - 12months.

After this ritual, feeding of food to the child begins.

In the beginning, well prepared food like kheer, khichdi, rice etc. is given.

7. अन्नप्राशन संस्कार

8. Chudakarma: When the hair of the head is removed for the first time, then it is called Chudakarma or Mundan Sanskar.

When the child is one year old, or at the age of three, or at the age of the fifth or seventh year, the child's hair is plucked.

This sanskar strengthens the child's head and sharpens the intellect.

Along with this, the germs sticking in the hair of the baby are destroyed, due to which the baby gets health benefits.

After coming out of the womb, only the hair given by the parents remains on the head of the child.

Cutting them leads to purification.

8. चूड़ाकरण संस्कार

9. Karnavedha : The meaning of Karnavedh Sanskar is piercing the ear.

There are five reasons for this, one - to wear jewelry. Second - Piercing the ear stops the bad effects of Rahu and Ketu according to astrology.

Third, it is acupuncture, due to which the flow of blood in the veins going to the brain starts to improve.

Fourth, it increases hearing power and prevents many diseases.

Fifth, it strengthens the sexual senses.

9. कर्णवेध संस्कार

10. Yagyopavit: When Child taking Birth that time child was pure and natural, but child starting to learn from childhood itself and at age of 5 years or more attached with various different types of thoughts, hence sending to learn or school for learning this is essential to purify the child such that child should reach to further Birth time itself for this purification Sanatan culture developed for Yagyopavit (Perform to Dwij)

Yagyopavit is also called 5 to 48 days Upanayan or Janeu Sanskar.

This is the compulsory activity before entering the School.

This is the Sanskar when children get Discipline in their Life to bring at Birth Stage Quality.

This is also an essential Sanskar for the Strong Democracy.

Every Individual on the basis of their Birth caste performs this sanskar.

Brahmin, Kshtriya and Vaishya who are taking birth to work for society have a compulsory requirement to be the Dwij as their mind is more creative and actionable, hence Guru is essential for them.

The person who is taking birth in Shudra Caste, they are not required to be Dwij, because their birth quality is to Serve the Society in peace as their mind is always in peace. But due to social disharmony these people reached a stage of Avid Yagami (Those who trying to be similar like others)

Upa means to pass and Nayan means to carry.

To be taken to the Guru means to perform the Upanayana ceremony.

There are three, Six and Nine sutras in the Janeu i. e. Yagnopavit.

These are the symbols of three deities - Brahma, Vishnu, Mahesh.

This sanskar gives the knowledge of Nature, strength, energy and radiance to the child. At the same time, a spiritual sense is awakened in him.

METHODOLOGY TO PERFORM UPNAYAN SANSKAR

Upnayan Sanskar is an old and Technical Sanskar which can change our Society in the Right Path. A few castes now follow this Sanskar and deliver it to the next Generation.

#Guru, #Asst. Guru & #Sevak must be a SAINT and practical personal and away from all Greeds and who can devote 12 days and Night with Children and teach the Children from 4AM and their age should be 65+and Asst. Guru age be 50+.

GURU must have 10 year experience as a Asst. Guru. Asst. Guru must have experience of min. 10yrs as a SEVAK.

SEVAK must be a person taken Upnayan Sanskar and following discipline from the last 10 years and without Greeds. Minimum age - 21 years.

Today we prepared a Guidelines in Stepwise such that we can improve the quality to our future generation, and present generation in Technical aspects such that our vision should run for a long time.

Plan is for a minimum of 11 days with ARYA MOUN, which is essential for UPNAYAN SANSKAR.

DAY - 1

Each PARENTS will make Puja of #KULDEVTA in Home and bring their son to Ashram till 2 PM with Light Clothes.

#Ashram will provide suitable Bed, Bed sheet and normal facility at ashram with suitable Chappal/Kharaw to all Children as guidelines of Guru & Asst. Guru.

5PM to 6PM - Dinner .

6PM - 7. 45PM - Introduction Classes by Guru & Asst. Guru. Delivery Speech for the programme of Upnayan Sanskar, Discipline of Ashram etc, start of #ARYA MOUN, and Dinner to Honorable Guest.

7. 45PM - 8. 15PM - Day & Next day Programme discussion and Sense, Brain & Intellect Pranayam by GURU.

DAY - 2

4AM - 4. 30AM - Wakeup and Become fresh with Bath. with help of Asst. Guru.

4. 30AM - 6. 30AM - Guru Bandana+Sarvangasan Pranayama+Self Surrender Pranayama+LIFE ENERGY PRANAYAM+Sense Brain & Intellect Control Pranayam (Class - I)

6. 30AM - 7AM - Breakfast

7AM - 11. 00AM - Preparation by Children of Marwa+Matkor+Haldi Kalash in guideline of GURU.

11. 00AM - 11. 45AM - Lunch

11. 45AM to 1. 30PM - Rest

1. 30PM - 3. 30PM - Organising of Marwa+Matkor+Haldi kalash

3. 30PM - 5. 30PM - Starting of Upnayan Sanskar+Ghrit Dhari+Puja of Satya Narayan Kath. Barua Dressing.

5. 30PM - 6. 00PM - Dinner to Barua

6. 00PM - 7. 45PM - Ayurveda & Bhakti Yog by Barua with GURU+Dinner to Honorable Guest.

7. 45PM - 8. 15PM - Day & Next day Programme discussion and Sense, Brain & Intellect Pranayam by GURU.

8. 15PM - 4AM - Rest.

DAY - 3

4AM - 4. 30AM - Wakeup and Become fresh with Bath with help of Asst. Guru.

4. 30AM - 6. 30AM - Guru Bandana+Sarvangasan Pranayama+Self Surrender Pranayama+LIFE ENERGY PRANAYAM+Sense Brain & Intellect Control Pranayam (Class - II)

6. 30AM - 7AM - Breakfast

7AM - 10. 00AM - BHICHHATAN - I (External decided by Guru)

10. 00AM - 11. 45AM - Preparation of Food & Lunch by Barua with GURU.

11. 45AM to 1. 30PM - Rest

1. 30PM - 3. 00PM - Practice of Self Surrender & Life Energy Pranayama under Asst. Guru.

3. 00PM - 4. 30PM - Practice of Sense, Brain & Intellect Pranayama under Asst. Guru.

4. 30PM - 6. 00PM - Preparation and Dinner to Barua under Guidance and with GURU.

6. 00PM - 7. 45PM - Ayurveda & Bhakti Yog by Barua under guidance of GURU+Dinner to Honorable Guest

7. 45PM - 8. 15PM - Day & Next day Programme discussion and Self Control Pranayam by GURU.

8. 15PM - 4AM - REST

Day - 4 (Class - III) and BHICHHATAN - II (External decided by GURU) , Rest similar as Day - 3

Day - 5 (Class - IV) , BICHHAWAN - III (External decided by GURU) , Rest similar as Day - 3

Day - 6 (Class - V) , BHICHHATAN - IV (External decided by GURU)

, Rest similar as Day - 3

Day - 7 (Class - VI) , BHICHHATAN - V (External decided by GURU) , Rest similar as Day - 3

Day - 8 (Class - VII) , BHICHHATAN - VI (External decided by GURU) , Rest similar as Day - 3

Day - 9 (Class - VIII) , BHICHHATAN - VII (External decided byGURU) , Rest similar as Day - 3

Day - 10 (Class - IX) , BHICHHATAN - VIII (External decided by GURU) , Rest similar as Day - 3

DAY - 11

4AM - 4. 30AM - Wakeup and Become fresh with Bath with help of Asst. GURU.

4. 30AM - 6. 30AM - SELF CONTROL MEDITATION (Class - X)

6. 30AM - 7AM - Breakfast

7AM - 10. 00AM - BHICHHATAN - IX from own family

10. 00AM - 11. 45AM - Preparation of Food & Lunch by Barua with GURU.

11. 45AM to 1. 30PM - Rest

1. 30PM - 4. 30PM - Providing UPNAYAN

SANSKAR to all Barua. (END OF ARYA MOUN)

4. 30PM - 6. 00PM - Preparation and Dinner by Barua under Guidance and with GURU.

6. 00PM - 7. 45PM - Ayurveda & Bhakti Yog by Barua under guidance of GURU+Dinner to Honorable Guest

7. 45PM - 8. 15PM - Day & Next day Programme and Self Control Pranayam by GURU.

8. 15PM - 4AM - Rest.

DAY - 12

4AM - 4. 30AM - Wakeup and Become fresh with Bath without help of Asst. GURU.

4. 30AM - 6. 30AM - SELF CONTROL MEDITATION (Class - XI)

6. 30AM - 7AM - Breakfast

7AM - 9. 00AM - Group Photographs and Discourse.

PARENTS WILL TAKE CARE OF CHILDREN.

END OF PROGRAMME.

10. उपनयन संस्कार

11. Vedarambh & Education: Under this the knowledge of Vedas is given to the person.

After Veda knowledge people get knowledge of their Birth Caste activity to strengthen the Economics of their family and Society or temple.

Practical schooling is required in society or Street temple to train the student in the right direction before 17 years of age.

Their mission was to teach the children in Gurukul after getting Upnayan Sanskar or School itself organizing the Upnayan Sanskar before entering the school.

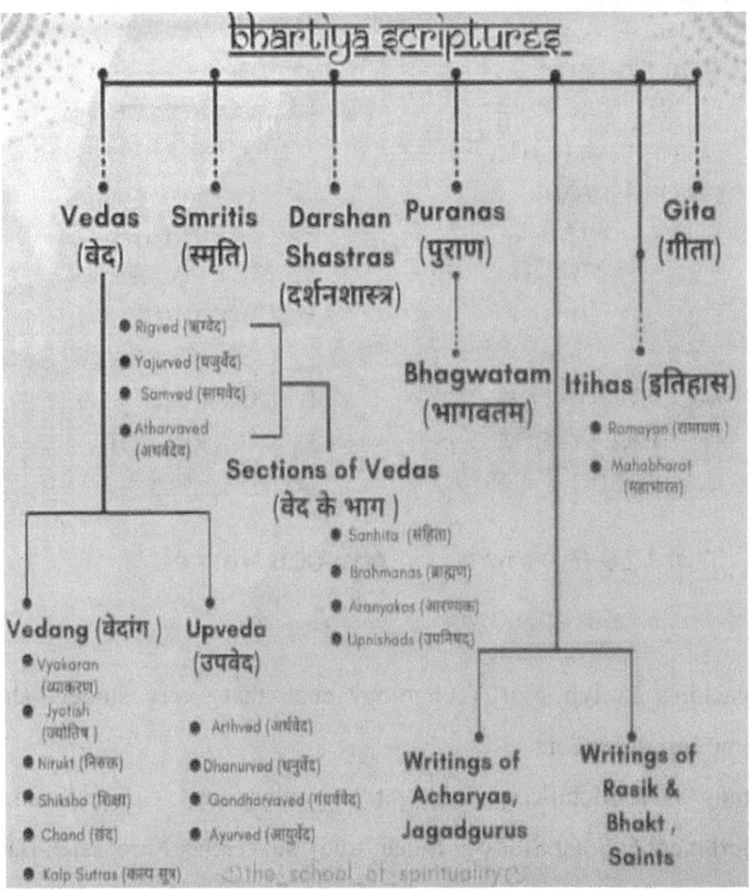

18 Puranas

18 Puranas:

Brahma Purana	10,000 Verses
Padma Purana	55,000 Verses
Vishnu Purana	23,000 Verses
Shiva Purana	24,000 Verses
Bhagavata Purana	18,000 Verses
Narada Purana	25,000 Verses
Markendya Purana	9,000 Verses
Agni Purana	15,400 Verses
Bhavishya Purana	14,500 Verses
Brahmavaivarta Purana	18,000 Verses
Linga Purana	11,000 Verses
Varaha Purana	24,000 Verses
Skanda Purana	81,100 Verses
Vaman Purana	10,000 Verses
Kurma Purana	17,000 Verses
Matsya Purana	14,000 Verses
Garuda Purana	19,000 Verses
Brahmand Purana	12,000 Verses
Total 18 Puranas	**400,000 Verses**

Teaching 25 types of Technology such that every student should become self dependent.

Study as 1. Metallergy 2. Flight 3. Navigation 4. Space Science 5. Enviornment 6. Solar Study 7. Lunar Study 8. Weather Forecast 9. Battery

10. Solar Energy 11. Technology of Day & Night 12. Space Research 13. Astronomy 14. Geography 15. Time 16. Geology and mining 17. Gravity 18. Solar Energy 19. Gems and Metals 20. Communication 21. Plane 22. Water vessels 23. Arms and Ammunitions 24. Zoology & Botany 25. Yagya or Material Science.

Gurukul also teaching the 25no. Commercial Education is as under-

1. Commerce 2. Agriculture 3. Animal Husbandry 4. Bird Keeping 5. Animal Training 6. Mechanics 7. Vehicle Designing 8. Gems 9. Jewellery Designing 10. Textile 11. Pottery 12. Metallurgy 13. Takshak 14. Dying 15. Khatawkar 16. Logistics 17. Architect 18. Cooking 19. Driving 20. Water Management 21. Data Entry 22. Animal Husbandry 23. Horticulture 24. Paramedical 25. Forestry Horticulture.

Apart of Sanatan or Democratic Law and All Lively New Technology.

Every student must get an offer from the Society or Street temple Government of 1 year training with Job offer.

Those who are not interested will get support from the Society or Street temple Government to start the Business.

Those who are interested in further study can go for further study, Society or Street temple Government will support them.

11.वेदारम्भ संस्कार

12. Samavartan: Samavartan Sanskar means to return again to their Home.

After receiving education from the ashram or gurukul, this sanskar was performed to bring the person back into the society.

It means preparing a celibate person psychologically for the struggles of life.

12. समावर्तन संस्कार

13. Marriage & Economic Life: It is necessary to get married at an appropriate age.

Marriage ceremony is considered to be the most important sacrament.

Under this, both the bride and the groom stay together and get married, taking a vow to follow the right path in front of Agni and water. Agni is the symbol of truth and purity. Water who remembers the things for a long time.

On the basis of Date of Birth, Place and Time the kundli Milan is the Ist step, after a matching marriage ceremony is held.

Marriage does not only contribute to the development of the universe, but it is also necessary for the spiritual and mental development of a person.

By this sanskar a person is also freed from the debt of the ancestors.

Marriage is also leading and strengthening their Economic Life.

Economic Life starts when Marriage takes place or when Men Women living together. Social Needs develop like organized Food, Water, Environment, Work and safety. Every activity needs valuable time to Perform.

Economy starts from Women, as women have the capacity to produce children.

Economic life itself generates the different types of business activity in Society and World.

Marriage is compulsory and essential for society, hence marriage should be organized at the age of 25 of Boy and 21 - 25 of Girl if both are in higher education, if not marriage should be organized at the age of just finishing the education and starting of earning life.

Guru has a special role in the marriage system.

Marriage of girls is now a day happening as wished by their Mother, Father and based on their today's education. Now Guru has least role in fixing Marriage.

People forget and insult the relationship, Guru and family in the name of education, wealth and reputation.

Development of Marriage System -

Caste is dependent on work.

Initially people were living in the jungle and performing sexual activity with anyone.

For safety, people started to live together and stayed in group. Women maintained multi relationships with different men, similarly Men also.

Forest is the place where we can get everything which is required for life, that is food, water, wood etc.

Further when people started to live together they cleaned the jungle to safeguard, due to this we loosen food and others.

At the same time people started to find alternatives to food.

Maximum people started to keep cattle and ox some people started to get food from the trees like from palm , Khajur, Mahua etc.

Further people started agriculture where safety from the jungle is found out.

Further development takes place and various work is started to safeguard.

The man who leads the troop or group is previously called King now they are called Leader.

Every person in this world has no caste; it is depending on the work they define.

Once upon a time everyone was tribal making sexual relations as desired, further development given the birth of Yadav , kurmi, Kishan, Pasi, Machhuara, etc. they started to stay in group and polygamy is common.

Further development divides kings, Dom, Chamar, Vaidya, Sant, kahar pandit, Lohar, etc. King is Polygamy and others are also under polygamy.

Further Leader, Engineer, Doctor, Lawyer , Accountant, Teacher under single relationship, The people who follow paigambar calling muslim have ancient tradition of tribal is Polygamy, people who follow jesus called christian marry in single relation, people who follow Lord budha calling buddhist marry only one etc.

We are all Human.

We have to follow the religion of Law of Nature and WE HAVE TO WORK TOGETHER TO SECURE OUR LIFE AS REQUIRED BY RUNNING SITUATION.

Mother has the main role in the birth of a child and the child has 95% purity of their mother, hence marriage must happen in relation itself.

As a girl can feel more safe in a family of mother genetics, hence every girl has first right to marry in the 2nd to 10th gene of mother (In Maternal Home.)

Case - I, Girl and Boy from different Caste, Religion and Gotra not matching (Love Marriage) - Child will born extraordinary, but differences in family will arise. Difficult to maintain as a Family.

Case - II, Girl and Boy from far relation, Gotra not matching - Child will born extraordinary, but differences in family will arise. Difficult to maintain as a Joint Family.

Case - III, Girl and Boy from far relation but in same Gotra and caste. Child will born Extraordinary, but differences in family will arise. Possibility to maintain as a Joint family system.

Case - IV, Girl and Boy from the same Gotra, Caste but more than 5th generation. Child will become Good, Differences in family will arise minimum and joint family will develop.

Case - V, Girl and Boy from same Gotra caste but 2nd to 4th Generation (Boy is child of Brothers or uncle or Grand father or Grand Grand father, mother of Girl and Boy is not own mausi) Child will born Average. Little differences will develop in family, but joint family system will develop easily.

Case - VI, Girl and Boy from same Gotra caste but from 2nd to 4th Generation (Boy is child of Brothers or uncle or Grand father or Grand Grand father, and mother of Girl and Boy is own Mausi) , Child will born Average. Genetic trouble will arise. No differences will develop in family.

Case - VII, Girl and Boy from same Gotra caste but from 2nd to 4th Generation (All Boy is child of Brothers or uncle or Grand father or Grand Grand father, should marry with single family Girl and mother of Girl and Boy is not own Mausi) , Child will born Good. Genetic trouble will not arise. No differences will develop in family.

Case - VIII, Girl and Boy from different Gotra caste or religion (All Boy is child of Brothers or uncle or Grand father or Grand Grand father, should marry with single family Girl, Girl sister, Mausi, Grand mother's sister. (Mother of Boy and Mother of Girl should not be Mausi) Child will born Extraordinary. Genetic trouble will not arise. No differences will develop in family.

Case - IX, A Women who lost their husband or A Man who lost their wife has right to go for 2nd marriage in same family with eligible Man or Women after family talk, In no case women should stay Bachelor in home. Man has to marry in relation of lost wife either sister or mausi or mausi

Girl. No differences will develop in family.

Case - X - Polygamy, Extra marital affair is common in various places, society and country is danger for mental peace, health and children. Children getting dis - affection from family. Family breaking, Joint family breaking even it leads to Death also.

Case - XI - On the basis of Sixteen Sanskar Marriage of All boys in one joint family should be in another all girl from joint family away from the same village or society on the basis of Horoscope Matching.

Ex - Successful family marriages are Ram, Laxman, Bharat and Shatrudhan with Daughter of Janak and his brother under guidance of GURU and their matching of Marriage Horoscope.

How Married can become a Successful -

Marriage is not only required in life to the birth of a new generation, but it also needs to understand and create the Joint family System strong hence marriage is need to happen in nearer but away of minimum such other than same house, society, Village, it also needs to understand each other deeply, and relationships as required by Nature.

13. विवाह संस्कार

14. Vanaprastha - It provides useful guidelines for peaceful departure from this world where the person comes for a limited period with a certain purpose.

ROUTINE -

Barefoot walking to a different TIRTH is the routine for this life.

Wake Up early in the morning at 4am.

Normally daily 12 KOS or 32 kilometer walking daily morning hour till

11am.

Eating twice Vegetarian food once before 12PM and 2nd before sunset.

Staying in a Temple or Ashram.

Performing morning puja and evening Meditation and some time talking with the public in afternoon time.

It is one's duty to pass on the mantle to the future generation without any attachment to one's own position.

It increases the Mangal Maitri.

14. वानप्रस्थ संस्कार

15. SANYAS ASHRAM -

Ashram means "a place of Work or spiritual shelter. " Each stage of life is not only a natural part of the journey from cradle to grave, but a time at which spirituality can be developed. The four varnas, accept ashrams as depicted in the table below:

	BRAHM ACARI	GRIHA STA	VANAPRAS THA	SANNY ASI
Shudra	no formal education	yes	no formal retirement	no formal sannyasa
Vaishya	yes	yes	no formal retirement	no formal sannyasa
Kshatriya	yes	yes	yes	no formal sannyasa
Brahmin	yes	yes	yes	yes

In Hinduism (SANATAN) renunciation or sanyasa is the true mark of spiritual life.

It is believed to be the simple and straightforward way to achieve moksha or liberation.

Truly speaking, in the context of sanyasa or renunciation, the word, "achieve, " is not the right word to use because "achieve" denotes materialism, seeking and striving for something, whereas in renunciation one has to give up worldly life and material possessions, and live without aiming for anything in particular, including the goal of salvation, liberation or union with God.

Having a purpose is important in worldly life, whereas not having any purpose is the central feature of renunciation or sannyasa in Hinduism.

A step which is the final path to increase the Mangal Maitri. His family is whole Nature.

TYPES OF SANYAS AND WORK -

Different types of Sanyas in the world are as under.

A. MONK

B. Mandir Pujari

C. Saint and performing Meditation in one place

D. Saint and traveling to Tirth E. Saint and performing meditation to construct the State or Country.

E. Munni

F. Father

G. Saint and performing meditation and running school, Temple and Health Center.

16. Activity After Death or Funeral rites -

There is three activity after Death is as under -

1. When Arihant takes Samadhi, it is required to be put under the Earth or Water Samadhi or Well Samadhi or Forest Samadhi as desired by Arihant.

2. When a Child takes Death, it is required to be put under the Earth.

3. Normal people who get death due to poor health or by accident or else the dead body is offered to the Fire.

15. सन्यास संस्कार

Thus sixteen sacraments are performed.

Antyashti Sanskar means funeral. After the death of a person i. e. renouncing the body, the dead body is offered to the fire.

Even today before the funeral procession, a fire is taken from the house by burning it.

16. अन्त्येष्टि संस्कार

7. Meaning of Gram Panchayat

What is Gram Panchayat? What is Gram Panchayat? What is a village? What is a small town? A village is formed and the population of a village is 2000 3000 5000, then a Gram Panchayat is arranged there which does the work of the development of street temples. Gram Panchayat does the same work. Builds up a good relationship with each other, how can we get married, have a relationship, be safe, have a business and other rituals, and become strong, then the work that people do there, select each other, some become the head, some become the leader. He becomes a Sarpanch and some committee is formed in him to resolve whatever problems he has in the Panchayat. In this Panchayat, which is formed in the middle of two - three villages, gradually a building is built, first a tree. Then the building is constructed, Havan is constructed, then how to keep the building safe there, then the temple is also constructed and there is Panchayat, people keep coming and going, people from outside also come to that Panchayat. In fact, there is a pot made there where education is also done, there are Acharyas etc. in the temples who give education, people in love, who have a wish on all Day, donate education there and arrangements are made to stay there. Arrangements for food are made in this way. Gram Panchayat is a very good system to solve our problems. Gram Panchayat is a very good system to solve the problems of two or three villages, which has relations with the temples of every state and works for the same. It is good work that Panchayat has its work for development and also take tax for the same thing. People give money to build the local roads there, to build a drain, to set up a pump, to prepare a canal to dump in the village and rivers. To build a bank so that water can reach the fields properly, to install sun energy panels so that the technicians can get light. In this way, many tasks keep going on in the Gram Panchayat. A bank is set up there so that people can deposit money there and withdraw it. And so that he can develop the area well.

8. Meaning of District Panchayat

Gram Panchayat is a primary stage of the state which went ahead of the temples and is a very good system created for conducting marriages. Furthermore, when people get married in other villages or in other Panchayats, the exchange of people starts from there. He wants to work beyond his knowledge, why don't we make him a district, here we create our own team and while making him, his place is also prepared for sitting at a district level. When the place is ready, then a meeting is also held there. They also give money so that it can be used for the development of the district and the people who work there, who work at the Panchayat level, form committees there who look at the development work, what is happening where and what is not happening. It also identifies whether what is necessary is happening or not, and other beneficial work is also done in it. If their living place is done, who will protect it, who will arrange it, who will take care of it, then the temple would have been built. Whether it is the priest who is present on his own or the learned priest who is in the temple of the State or the temple of the Gram Panchayat of the village, but the scholars who live there are appointed there, they take care of them and serve them. Answer: If there is a temple then there will also be a monastery. Even the work of studying is done there, don't school people, accommodation arrangements are made, in this way it gets developed and a very big sub - centre is formed, people in the district give money and build big schools there, build colleges. We build an institution, many websites are developed in the area and a hospital is built there so that our people do not go far away and in case of any emergency, they can be easily treated at the district level.

9. Meaning of State Panchayat

District Panchayat later takes the form of State Panchayat. In State

Panchayat, those who do the work of District Panchayat or the work of Gram Panchayat or the work of State Panchayat, all together form a committee and run the state. Now see, when we start running the state, then who will look after the arrangements there? All the arrangements are made there, first of all the Mahant is appointed, a temple is built, the Math is built there, people are arranged for the police station, food arrangements are made there. Then there is a discussion about security. Arrangements for security have been made. There will be discussion about going to the hospital. Arrangements have been made in hostels. Arrangements have been made for schools. Arrangements for universities have been made. Business arrangements have been made. Arrangements for the same are made, so it is necessary, isn't it?

10. Meaning of Country Panchayat

Country is a slightly advanced form of State Panchayat. Country is for the entire country. The people who work on it are those who are from the state or district level. Those from the village level reach there and then a committee is formed in which people discuss. They regularly discuss about the problem in different corners of the country and see its safety and security. A big temple is built in which Acharyas staying there, they see the whole system and sometimes a Math is made so that more and more people can take education there. A health center is built by the people of unity, if possible, anyone of the country who has problems can go there and get better health. Many big schools and colleges are established in the country at different affordable prices, especially where committees are formed so that the people of the country can get better health. People from every corner can come and take admission there, it becomes the center of the entire business so that the website can be good for the entire country. This is a very big thing. Making it very thoughtfully is good for any country.

11. Economy of Twenty Four Hour - Twelve Hour - One Hour Concept & Responsibility of Sanatan Sangha.

Economy starts when a man is born, it happens at this time, every man, every living being is a lesson in economy, when he comes into a family and builds a house, then even more, the economy increases as a family is formed, there is a need for food, some will say something, some will eat something, there is a need to drink water. There is a need for houses, there is a need for light so that people can live well, all this is a part of the economy, how will it be achieved, it is achieved by working, it is achieved from the fields, by working in the fields, people can also earn or earn a lot. If people have money, then rich people have money. Those who are rich people, now see here, when we go ahead of the economy, another one of ours will also go, where if we go ahead of the family, then we will meet for an hour anywhere and then there. A discussion takes place, a temple is built, different people do business, different people engage in different types of business according to 12 hours, so this is your lesson of economy, whatever formation is sometimes done in the temple, all the same in the temple of receipt. People, if there is any locality like a street, there is a locality which is built on a temple, when there are 500 to 1000 people there, people stop comfortably for an hour or half an hour, when they do it and gradually build a temple. Permission is granted and if a person starts giving one hour daily in the temple or starts giving 12 hours daily in his home, whatever is the income, deposit it on you and give one hour.

Imagine if there are 1000 families in the street then the family has become 200. If a family gives one hour at a street temple, then they have 200 hours there. All family of who does not have □ 1. one people can pay Rs. 10. Apart from that, the puja, recitation and other 16 rituals that they do. If there are people, then the money goes there, in this way, it is a big starting point of our economy. Who is there, the temple in our street becomes the biggest money maker because temple will receive the 200 hours daily and 200 hours daily multiplied becomes 6000 hours per months. Think of it this way. How much would be done in a year, then this is the hour of work and the one who gives □ 1, all this is of Minimum Rs. 200 as a donation.

A CASE STUDY -

CONCEPT OF SOCIAL ENGINEERING AND SAFETY OF PROFESSIONAL -

UNDERSTANDING OF MAHARISHI, RISHI, MUNI, SAINT, SANT, ENGINEER, DOCTOR, LAWYER OR CA, ARCHITECTURE, GRIHSWAMINI, GRADUATE, MATRIC, NON MATRIC AND CONSTITUTION OF BHARAT is as under -

In Social Engineering Professional Safety is the major requirement of the Society.

Society is developing in its own way as per prevailing conditions in society and various qualities are developing in a proportionate manner.

World and every element in the world is the formation and combination of 9 elements: Earth, Water, Light, Wind, Ether, Time, Space, Mind and Soul.

Only one mission of every creature's life is to be in Mangal Maitri for 24x7x365x various years.

Indian social Engineering depends on the following universal designation based on the acquired Magal Maitri.

By Birth there is only three caste is as under -

1. Man

2. Women

3. Trans - Gender

Details

Caste is dependent on work.

Initially people were living in the jungle, For safety people started to live together.

Forest is the place where we can get everything which is required for life, that is food, water, wood etc.

Further when people started to live together they cleaned the jungle to safeguard, due to this we loosen food and others.

At the same time people started to find alternatives to food.

Maximum people started to keep cattle and ox some people started to get food from the trees like from palm , Khajur, Mahua etc.

Further people started agriculture where safety from the jungle is found out.

Further development takes place and various work is started to safeguard.

The man who leads the troop or group is previously called King now they are called Leader.

Every person in this world has no caste; it is depending on the work they define.

Once upon a time everyone was tribal, further development given the birth of Yadav , kurmi, Kishan, Pasi, Machhuara, etc.

Further development divides kings, Dom, Chamar, Vaidya, Sant, kahar pandit, Lohar, etc.

Further Leader, Engineer, Doctor, Lawyer , Accountant, Teacher , The people who follow paigambar calling muslim, people who follow jesus called christian, people who follow Lord budha calling buddhist etc.

We are all Human.

We have to follow the religion of Law of Nature and WE HAVE TO WORK TOGETHER TO SECURE OUR LIFE AS REQUIRED BY RUNNING SITUATION.

Working together needs Mangal Maitri meaning extreme positivity in mind.

Mangal Maitri is the prime requirement of society such that different people can work together, But in the present day it is missing.

We have a holiday to have FUN, while it is needed for SADHNA.

What is a Holiday?

Holiday is a Common day of Leave after continuous working so that people can get recharged.

There is a holiday on Saturday, Sunday. What is the use of this Holiday?

People travel here and there and enjoy LIFE which is not only disturbing the Peace condition it also not suitable for the gain of ENERGY.

Next working day people are not interested in work. In Present Development of society it is essential to have a public Holiday to perform the Sadhana not to spoil the day to enjoy.

Enjoy destroying the Mangal Maitri Condition.

Hence preferable Holiday for Country should be based on Sadhna.

Now the question arises, when we can perform Sadhna. Right time is a junction of two seasons causing the effect of various viruses and diseases.

Hence following Leave should be organized in world for better health and prosperity is as under

1. 4 Navratri/Upnayan Sanskar sadhna/Sangha Sadhna/ Vipasana Sadhna/SEASON CHANGING SADHNA in ASIN (Rainy - Autumn/Winter) , MAGH (Winter - Vasant)) , CHAIT (Vasant - Summer) , ASADH (Summer - Rainy) Amavasya to Dasmi - 40 Days

2. Amavasya Sadhan - 12 Days (A day when water percentage fall down from 72%, it needs a Sadhna to Water)

3. Purnima Sadhna - 12 Days (A day when water percentage increases from 72%, it still needs a Sadhna of water to increase the energy in the human body.)

4. Holi and Holika/Vipasana Sadhna on Purnima Falgun & Chaitya Ist - 1 Days

5. Diwali and Laxmi/Vipassana Sadhana Chaturdasi & Amavasya karthik - 1 Days

6. Uttarayan Kaalchakra (Changing of Movement of SUN) /Makar Sankranti/ Upnayan Sanskar Sadhna/Sangh Sadhna/ Vipassana and Sadhna (5Jan - 16Jan) - 1 Days preferable on (Dev Uthni Ekadashi if it comes) For Expert - 11 days and Special Sadhna from (21 December - 16Jan) - 27days. And Extraordinary Sadhna from (08 December - 26 jan)

7. Dakshinayan Kaalchakra (Changing of Movement of SUN from Cancer to Capricorn) /Cancer or Karka Sankranti/Upnayan Sanskar Sadhana/Sangh Sadhna/Vipassana and Sadhna (5 July - 16 july) - 1 days preferable for Normal People on (Dev Sayani Ekadasi if it comes) For

Expert - 11 days and Special Sadhna from (21 June - 16JJuly) - 27days and Extraordinary Sadhna from (08 June to 26 July) - 48days

8. Chhath Vrat Suryopasana/Vipassana Kartik & Chaitya 4th, 5th and 6th day - 6 Days

9. Independence (15th August) & Gantantra (26th Jan) Divas Sadhna/Vipassana - 2 Days.

Total of 76 Days of Sadhna for Normal People.

Or 74+11+11=96 Days of Expert SADHNA.

Or 74+27+27=128 Days of Special SADHNA.

Or 74+48+48=170 days of Extra ordinary Sadhna.

In one year SADHNA of 76 days for normal people and 96 days for Expert People , 128 days for Special SADHNA for Rishi and 170 days of Extraordinary Sadhna for Rishi and Maharishi is a compulsory requirement to gain natural Energy to create the Country SMART.

This above Auspicious day is required to be in peace not to run the mike or unwanted gathering rather should be for SADHNA only.

Market should also be designed such that PEACE should not be disturbed. Vehicle movement should be restricted.

Vehicles should be allowed which does not create NOISE or SMOKE etc means only Electric Vehicle or Rickshaw or Walking should be allowed.

It is well known that from morning 2. 30AM to 4AM Nature performs the MEDITATION.

From 4AM to 6. 30AM - All Creatures and Human beings Performing the Meditation.

From 6. 30AM to 12AM - Working Period.

Peace Conditions always increasing the Efficiency.

From 12PM to Sunset - Hard Work Period.

Peace condition energizes the Body to perform effectively.

Mike sound, Sound Pollution should not be allowed.

Mike should allowed for VED KATHA YAGYA, UPNISHAD KATHA YAGYA, PURAN Katha YAGYA, Ramayan Katha YAGYA, GITA Katha YAGYA, if every family is agreed.

From Sunset to 8PM - Creatures returning from their work and discussing the day.

This is the time of Collective Gayan, Music etc in one place.

If all people agreed then Mike may ON.

From 8PM to 2. 30AM Rest and Sleeping Period. All Creatures return home and take rest and sleep, hence this is also the period of REST such as all creatures should gain the perfect SLEEP to energize their LIFE.

HENCE PEACE is essential to create the Smart Society.

TRADITION, DAVA AND DARU is an essential tool to reach a healthy condition.

Quantity is per the Peace Condition of Life. Example - In Bihar region HARIA, MAHUA AND TARI are the common and traditional JUICES which are prepared in house to use such as keep the healthy body.

Such as in Summer, HARIA is very good for health and Mahua is a good juice for the Winter Season and Tari for every season.

Eating Water Rice in morning is a tradition of BIHAR for the Summer Season from Holi Festival and Eating Sattu in daytime is another tradition of BIHAR for Summer Season.

Eating Chura Dahi in the morning is a tradition of BIHAR for the Rest season other than Summer Season

STAGES IN LIFE -

Maharishi - The sages who reach their higher level of Mangal Maitri are called Maharishis. Like Shankaracharya, Lord Budha etc.

Sage - Sage is the author of Vedic hymns, which is possible due to hundreds of penances and meditation.

Muni - One who attains knowledge by practicing spiritual practice and remaining silent. Like Jain Muni.

Sadhu - The person who performs spiritual practice is called a sadhu.

Saints - Peaceful people practice peace. practice the truth. Like Sant Ravidas, Kabirdas, Tulsidas

Ignorant - People who are incomprehensible because of ignorance and intense fickleness. Today people of these qualities are found in abundance.

Shudra - One who serves quietly. Mukti is confirmed if they follow quality otherwise due to fickleness next birth in Vaishya, Kshatriya or Brahmin/Diwana. There is no need of a Guru, the Guru of a Shudra is the real nature.

Vaishya - One who does business calmly. Mukti is confirmed if they are following birth discipline otherwise Development of spasticity, next birth in Shudra, Kshatriya or Brahmin/Diwana. Because of fickleness, the need for a Vedic teacher.

Kshatriya - Protector carrying fickleness. If quality is followed of birth mukti is confirmed but Vedic Guru is always needed because of extreme fickleness. Due to differences in birth quality, Next birth should be in Brahmin, Vaishya, Shudra or Diwana.

Brahman - The storehouse of knowledge, penance and meditation full of playfulness. And in the end engage in service. Mukti is confirmed if they follow birth quality otherwise Next birth in Brahmin, Diwana or Shudra . Brahmin needs Continuous a Vedic Guru because of extreme fickleness.

Diwana - People full of fickleness and ignorance are engrossed in their mite. Lack of concentration, uncontrollable wandering and thinking is their work. Roaming life, next birth Brahman or Kshatriya or attainment of salvation.

The constant need of a Vedic Guru to reduce the effects of excessive fickleness and ignorance.

AvidYagami - When the natural quality of birth changes due to the influence of society and ignorance of birth, then human beings become AvidYagami. Continuous need of Vedic Guru. Next birth Vaishya Kshatriya or Brahmin or Deewana is fixed.

There is no need for a guru for peaceful beings. Nature is their teacher. A Vedic Guru is needed to bring restlessness to peace.

To do business in the Vedic way, Vedic vocational education is fixed for all eighteen years.

Playfulness is necessary for the construction and protection of society and peace is necessary for ready love.

Maharishi and Rishi are knowledgeable by penance of Vedic secrets, and peace and meditation are necessary for Muni. And it is possible for everyone to become a saint by meditation and a saint by just peace.

Ignorance is a tendency of man from birth, there is no need to do anything for it.

In Ayurvedic Sanatan Hindu Rashtra India, only Maharishi is eligible for President as per unwritten constitution and Rishi, Sage and Sadhu for Governor and Sadhu and Saint for Prime Minister, Minister and Chief Minister.

All the scholars should try to become the form of Muni. Rest is suitable for the person who is in Ignorance.

Birth is the cause of development of will in previous life. If cause will end Birth cycle will end. Nothing is permanent in the world, everything has to be destroyed.

Jatkarma on the basis of astrology is essential to each being while Upnayan Sanskar is not essential for the person who is pure Sudra (A person in always peace) , Even Sudra also required Upnayan to understand life deeply and Vedic Education with meditation to reach a stage of PEACE as mostly Sudra changing to Avidyagami due to social disharmony.

Marriage is a system which helps to create a peaceful, high morale, stable joint family to perform Business, Safety and Living peacefully.

Antyeshti is essential to perform on the basis of being desired, but destroying the dead body in Agni should be common while Water Samadhi, Earth Samadhi depends on their condition of mental health, Social and personal and special requirements.

To destroy the attachment with the person it is essential to go for Agni samadhi. Mainly family people should follow agni Samadhi exception incase of specific diseases go for Water Samadhi or Earth Smadhi or throwing in Jungle.

External Safety and Sixteen Sanskar are predominant in Life.

Social Engineering is the 100% connectivity with the Sixteen Sanskar and External Safety.

Latest Development of Society should not be discarded.

The Latest Development is as under -

Maharishi, Rishi, Muni, Saint, Sant, Shudra, Vaishya, Kshtriya, Brahmin,

Deewana, Avidyagami and Ignorant is the natural development of human beings in Society.

Apart from this due to the latest education following professionals are available in Society.

Engineer - Those who completed the Engineering Education.

Lawyer or CA - Those who completed Law Education or Chartered Accountancy.

Architect - Those who are qualified Architect.

Doctor - Those who are Qualified Doctors in Ayurveda, Homeopathy, Allopathy and Naturopathy.

Grihswamini - Those who are experts of Home Kitchen health Laboratory and support to Family Health.

Graduate - Those who are Graduate from the other Subject.

Matriculation - Those who qualified as a Matriculation.

Non Matric - Those who have no knowledge of writing and reading or who have not passed the Matriculation.

Right utilization of this development will lead the country in extraordinary Development.

12. Conclusion and Further Study

Sanatan Sangh Parivar - 24 hours 12 hours and 1 hour is really a wonderful.

All this denoting to AYURVEDIC SANATAN HINDU RASTRA AKHAND BHARAT/WORLD as Ayurvedic means whole world is Ayurvedic, I am ayurvedic, you are ayurvedic. All creatures in this world is Ayurvedic. Women is much more as Women is connected with the Nature, Children connected with the Navel of Women and run by respiration.

Women and Man both are the product of nature which is the product of ZERO is as under -

Soul, Mind, Space, Time, Akash, Air, Agni, Water and Earth

Women is the Barren nature and Man is the executor who is developing the vibration in women due to integration and differentiation and creating the various population on the Earth (In form of visible form with smell) , Water (In visible and water form in frm of taste) , Agni (In different vision) , Air (In various form of touch either cold or Hot) , Akash (In form of different different Sound) , Time (In form of Vibration) , Space (In form of different Vacuum) . Mind (In different form of thought) and Soul (In different form of life) and ZERO (Means creator of Universe.)

SANATAN PARAMPARA - The Culture which developing naturally in WORLD. When People was alone, they started to live together for safety of each other and children. Later at one place various number of family living and for their own benefit meeting one place and creating temple in different different form and developing the pujari by own. Futher it develop with various Karyakarta to Gram Panchayat with Math and Mandir, District Panchayat with Math and Mandir, State Panchayat with Math and Mandir and Country Panchayat with Math and Mandir.

HINDU RASTRA - The Land from Himalaya to Kanniyakumari is called Hindu Rastra.

This happening in life by own way which indicates to create the Democratic Constitution or Sanatan Constitution.

www.ingramcontent.com/pod-product-compliance
Lightning Source LLC
LaVergne TN
LVHW031427170726
843492LV00009B/2886

* 9 7 8 8 1 9 7 5 9 9 6 6 8 *